CHURCH, LAW AND SOCIETY

CHURCH, LAW AND SOCIETY

by

Gustaf Aulén

BISHOP OF
STRÄNGNÄS, SWEDEN

INTRODUCTION BY NELS F. S. FERRÉ

NEW YORK
CHARLES SCRIBNER'S SONS
1948

To
THE RIGHT REVEREND

EIVIND BERGGRAV
BISHOP OF OSLO

True witness to the Light
in the age of darkness
and
True defender of Justice

PREFACE

UNDOUBTEDLY the Church in recent times has become more and more concerned about her responsibility for Society. Isolationist tendencies still appear. Nevertheless they are doomed. There is no place for social isolation in an age of world wars and atomic bombs.

What then is the duty of the Church? What are her responsibilities? It seems that the theological treatment of these questions has been exposed mainly to two dangers. Sometimes the social activity of the Church has been maintained at the sacrifice of her central message. Other times the Church has unfolded utopian ideas and asserted untenable presumptions. The responsibility of the Church cannot be too energetically emphasized. At the same time the Church must cautiously keep away from all false pretensions. The present situation demands a thorough self-examination of the Church.

Such a self-examination must carefully consider what it means that the Church has been entrusted not only with the gospel but also with the law of God. The viiiPREFACE

nature of her responsibility cannot be understood without an explanation of the meaning, place and importance of this law. If the Church does not possess a clear conception of the function of the law, her attitude necessarily will be uncertain and wavering, and her most primary responsibilities will be obscured.

Law and justice belong together. Our generation has witnessed the most disastrous breakdown of justice. We know now better than ever that justice is the foundation of all human relationship. Certainly the Church has various duties to perform in relation to Society. But her primary duty must be to strengthen the sense of true justice, according to the will of God as expressed in the law of the Creator.

This little book contains the Hewett lectures delivered in April and May, 1947. Sending it out I wish to express my deep thankfulness to the Trustees of the Hewett Foundation: President Henry P. Van Dusen of Union Theological Seminary, New York; Dean Vaughan C. Dabney of Andover Newton Theological School, Newton Centre, Massachusetts; and Dean Charles L. Taylor, Jr., of Episcopal Theological School, Cambridge, Massachusetts. To them as well as to their faculties I owe the greatest debt of gratitude.

GUSTAF AULÉN

The Bishop's Residence,
Strängnäs, Sweden,
October, 1947.

CONTENTS

INTRODUCTION

THERE can be no question that the relation between the Christian Church and Society is today a crucial issue for all Christians who think and care. The world trembles on the brink of destruction. A confused, weary-worn, and disintegrating civilization is wistfully looking for help in which it can believe and trust. The Church should come to its aid, both by supplying creative energy and moral directives. Yet the Church generally neither understands nor accepts its own nature and high mission. For the Church to understand itself, its nature and message, and then relate itself effectively to the world in general is more and more felt to be a prime necessity.

Historically, as Bishop Aulén points out, there have been two centrally defective relationships between Protestantism and Society: pietism and modernism. Pietism, based on a personal, evangelical experience, either withdrew ineffectively from the corruptions of the world or else tried to change it outright, considering converted men directly capable of the task. In one way lay sterility; in the other, idealistic pretension.

On one side lay passivity; on the other, perfectionism. Modernism, on the other hand, sold out the Gospel by secularizing it, thus shearing it of its power. In no case was real light and power brought to bear on the central issues and critical situations. As Bishop Aulén himself writes: "The relation of the Church and Society has been exposed to two main temptations. The first is the temptation to passivity and indifference, the second to false pretensions and to embracing Utopian and illusionary ideals."

But a new theological orientation in our day is making possible the understanding of a more effective relation. This orientation is due to a return to the deepest intentions of Reformation theology and consequently also of biblical theology. Especially important in this new theology is its stress on the centrality of God's love, and on the Church rather than on the individual as the primary recipient of it. Salvation by the love of God is here seen to be through the new self as a member of the body of Christ. This Christian fellowship is thus the key to the relation between Christianity and the world.

The fearful depths of horror and lawlessness in the modern warring world have particularly awakened the Church to a new responsibility for the world. Nazism especially made the Church aware of the problem of justice and its basic nature in the civil order. Its universality and majesty had to be affirmed even unto the prolonged persecution of the Church, as, for instance, in Norway, President Öhrn of the Baptist theological school in Oslo has told how his people came to see that the salt of the Gospel and the meat of the world could not be kept in two separate barrels. They had to be mixed and the salt put in with the meat! The Church, it was seen, had to defend more than the right to preach the Gospel; it had also to defend the right of sovereign justice in the life of Society.

Yet the Christian understanding of justice cannot be founded on human rationality, on natural law, on inalienable rights or on intrinsic human dignity. The Church has to found it on the law of God as a dynamic, creative force in all of history. In the realm of redemption the Gospel abolished the law, to be sure, but *only* there. The law of justice remains applicable and active in all other realms of life. The love of God is the essence of the law of justice, and, therefore, for a Christian to be Christian and for the Church to be the Church, they must care concretely for the world in all its needs. Charity is not enough. A basic necessity is the preservative and constructive maintenance and development of the law of justice. Love and justice cannot be torn apart, as far as the responsibility of the Church for Society goes, without damaging them both. The Church that would be responsible for the world is itself under this majestic judgment of perfect dynamic justice and cannot, therefore, ever see itself truly in the light of the full implications of the Gospel without becoming both responsible for the world and at the same time without self-righteousness.

When the place of the law is rightly seen by the Church in its honest self-examination, the Church can become responsibly concerned for and with the world in their common problems without passivity, on the one hand, and without perfectionism, on the other. Such a Church will not defensively isolate itself nor claim all goodness for itself, but with a generous heart and a steady eye will both make its good confession as to its nature and message and also in humbleness of heart, before God and man, co-operate with the constructive forces of Society to maintain as far as possible a dynamic, constructive order of justice and common civil life generally.

This is certainly no summary of this important book. It is interesting, however, to note that a viewpoint like this is sponsored by one of the leading Lutheran theologians of the world. A church historian, after hearing one of these chapters, said to me that Bishop Aulén "has thrown historic Lutheranism clear out the window." (Be that as it may, surely the modification is at one point only, and itself not new to historic Lutheranism.) What a valuable statement, in any case, this book is, coming from a leading Lutheran thinker and churchman before and after the Assembly of the World Council of Churches at Amsterdam! Many will say that Bishop Aulén has grafted distinctly Calvinistic features onto his historic Lutheran position. What stress, for instance, is placed on obedience as a conditioning factor of the Christian faith and life! How also the traditionally rather distinct division of spheres between Church and State is repudiated! But here comes the rub: historic Lutheranism insofar as it has really yielded to the temptations of which it has been accused, especially in the case of the German Church, was never true to all of Luther. Thus Bishop Aulén, for his understanding of the relation between Church and Society, especially as mediated by the Law, goes right back to Luther, citing key passages from him, and back, indeed, to the deepest intention and drive of the New Testament thought. These features of the book are utterly important and will cause serious discussion in many thoughtful and influential circles. They are exactly what we need from Lutheranism as we enter more fully into ecumenical discussion.

This volume, too, will come as another evidence of the vitality of Swedish theology. Within the last few years the Swedish theological movement, known mostly as the *Agape* movement or as the "Lundensian School," has produced a number of significant books that have girdled the globe with their vital influence. One of the best known of these works is Anders Nygren's *Agape and Eros,* in three volumes. But a large and vigorous translation project is now under way that will shortly see translated into English a large number of further significant works of modern Swedish theology. Then something of its importance will begin to be understood. *Church, Law and Society* may be the first acquaintance that many readers will have with this movement and will be of no little importance even on that account. This volume is also important to those who know Swedish theology well, because it fills a gap where the movement was particularly lacking.

The thoughtful reader will find the analysis of this book exceptionally keen, sturdy and Christian. Naturally it leaves many problems still unanswered. Especially we should like to have seen the Bishop discuss particular issues more fully, such as participation in war in a world like this that seems to be destroying itself through it. Should the Christian help prepare for war under such circumstances? *Just when* must we obey God rather than men? Yet the general principles are here, from a central Christian perspective, and we cannot expect to have too many concrete, existential questions answered for us by works of this nature.

Numerous people know Bishop Aulén mostly from his book, *Christus Victor*. Many theologians and New Testament scholars consider this work one of the very best in the field. Yet his more comprehensive systematic writings are only now being translated. *Church, Law and Society* reveals the same careful analyzer of Christian teachings discussing a most important topic for our day. It gives me real pleasure, therefore, to be privileged to introduce this book, for I am convinced that it will make a real contribution to our thinking and future discussions—and, I hope, what is most important, to *future action* on the part of the Church.

NELS F. S. FERRÉ

CHURCH, LAW AND SOCIETY

I

TOWARDS A REALISTIC AND RADICAL INTERPRETATION OF CHRISTIANITY

THE question about the relationship between Church and Society raises innumerable problems. We are confronted with problems as to the judicial system, social questions, family, education, science, art, culture as a whole, international questions of different kinds. We could also have reason to consider the position of the Church in the life of Society, her organization, her freedom and her possibilities to act according to the mandate entrusted to her. In fact, there scarcely exists any question of importance that could not be seen from the point of view of the relationship between Church and Society.

However, it is not my intention to deal in detail with all these different and difficult problems. My main purpose will be to speak about the duty and responsibility of the Church. It may, perhaps, be necessary to emphasize the word Church. It is not my intention to deal foremost with the question as to how Christians as individuals may act in reference to the different social, economic, political and cultural problems. It is

1

rather to examine the obligations of the Church as such, to present the reasons why the Church cannot stand apart from the life of Society without failing in her duty, and to state what indeed her responsibility means.

In the title of this book the word Law has been placed between Church and Society. Obviously that means, according to my opinion, that the Law is an important link between Church and Society. In order not to be misunderstood I must immediately add two remarks. First, it would of course be quite wrong to divide the Christian message and to speak about the Law of God as something separated from that message. Certainly, the Christian message is a unity. because it is altogether an expression of the will and mind of God, of His Love. But at the same time this unitary message must be seen from different points of view, as Law and as Gospel. Secondly, it would also be quite wrong to say that all connections between Church and Society must go through the Law. Nevertheless, the Law here has an importance not to be overlooked, and in the present situation it seems to be rather a necessary theological task to make clear what exactly is the function of the Law. Such an investigation is in fact necessary, because theology in the last centuries often has had a tendency to reduce or to obscure the position and function of the Law, to push it away or to confuse the Gospel with the Law and thus to moralize the Gospel.

Later I shall have many opportunities to discuss in greater detail the sense of the Law. As a preliminary determination it may be enough to say that the Law here is obviously thought of as the Law of God, that it is considered as a universal Law, and finally that it is conceived not in a static or abstract way as a collection of fixed rules and paragraphs, but instead of that as a dynamis, as a force working everywhere in human life. That means that the activity of the Law is not confined only to the Church. It is working also outside the boundaries of the Church, as sure as the living God is working throughout the universe. But at the same time, the full sense of the universal Law is revealed to the Church, and therefore it acts as a compass, the deflexions of which the Church can read in "the word of God."

The Church has been entrusted with the word of God. The word of God exists as Gospel and as Law. The Church is born to life through the Gospel, while the Law, as the Law of the Creator, was already in existence before the appearance of the Church. Indubitably, the main duty and privilege of the Church is to proclaim the Gospel. But that does not mean that the validity of the Law should have ceased with the appearance of the Gospel. When St. John says that the Law was given through Moses, but grace and truth came by Jesus Christ, or when St. Paul says that Christ is the end of the Law, that does not mean a general dethronement of the Law. It means that salvation is given only by the grace of God, and that it cannot be found by way of the Law. So far Christianity has put the Law out of function. But that does not mean that the Law would no longer have any function. On the contrary, it elucidates its real function. As expressing the will of God, the Law is holy and remains holy. Its validity and functions are unbroken in the dominion that really belongs to the Law. The Law is no way to God, but it is the way to all human relationship.

When looking back at the relationship between Church and Society in the last centuries, we certainly find many various attitudes and positions. Nevertheless, in the midst of all these variations it may be possible to discern two main types. One type has its origin in pietism and is stamped by its view of Christianity. In arguing against the "intellectualism" of orthodoxy, pietism would most strongly emphasize the personal character of Christianity, the necessity of conversion, of the new birth and the new life. It would draw a very sharp dividing line between Christians and "the world." From this starting-point, pietism could tread two different ways. One way led to passivity as regards the life and problems of Society. "The whole world lieth in wickedness," therefore the first duty of the Christian must be to withdraw from "the world" and keep uninfected by the evil. On the other side, the pietistic view could also lead to an intense activity. The Christians being changed have to work to change the world. They have the qualifications that make such a work possible. As far as the Law is here concerned, the idea is that the Law of God is being fulfilled through converted and changed men. If man has not been converted and born again, he cannot do anything "good," but being born again he has thereby been qualified to perform the will of God as given in His Law and written in the hearts of the faithful. Therefore, the Christian life is more or less considered from a perfectionist point of view.

The second type appears in different varieties. We find it fully manifested already in the theology of the Enlightenment, and then continued in another form in the religious modernism of the nineteenth century, that may be said to be the leading theology of that time. This type has nothing of the exclusiveness that characterized pietism. On the contrary, its tendency was to unite Christianity and humanity. Trying to realize this program, theology found its basis not only in the Christian message but also in the idealistic philosophy. As regards the conception of man, a distinction was then usually made between the higher, spiritual, "divine" part and the lower, sensual part of man, the latter being the seat of sin. When thus the "divine" part of man was considered superior to sin and therefore as the connecting point between God and man, "salvation" chiefly meant a strengthening of the spiritual power of man. Also in the outlook of history we meet a similar idealization. While pietism could have a perfectionist view of the Christian life, the humanizing theology of religious modernism would see history as such from a perfectionist and very often also an evolutionist point of view, as a progressive realization of the Kingdom of God in this world. It was thought that the Law of love would more and more penetrate and govern human society and so realize the ideal brotherhood. Obviously, this conception was a modernizing reinterpretation and at the same time a moralization of Christianity, a confusion of Gospel and Law. When the Kingdom of God was thus primarily apprehended as an ethical-cultural ideal being realized within the boundaries of this world and this time, that in fact meant a secularization of the Christian idea of the Realm of God.

In the last centuries, the conception of the Church's relation to Society has chiefly been determined either by a pietistic, more or less traditional, or by a modernist and humanizing, more or less reinterpreting view of Christianity. In the long contest between these two views, supremacy has alternated. In the life of the Church the more traditionalistic view of pietism has often prevailed over its rival. But from the point of view of theological research, pietism on the whole has been the weaker party, mainly on account of its traditionalism and its more or less biblical fundamentalism. However, in our days neither of the two types can be said to represent the leading theology. Certainly, they have not disappeared. They may still be influential in many quarters. Nevertheless, we must ask if we are not on the way to pass a turning-point in the history of theology. There are at least many signs indicating sincere endeavors towards a more realistic and radical approach to Christianity, different both from the traditional pietism as well as from the modernist reinterpretation.

In recent times you will find signs of such a new orientation everywhere in different countries, in America as well as in England, on the European continent and in the Scandinavian countries. The change in the theological atmosphere may have appeared earlier in one Church than in another, it may have a clearer outline in one country than in another. The theological expositions may differ as much regarding the positive statements as regarding the controversy. Nevertheless, it cannot be denied that the current flows in a quite definite direction, different from the older currents.

The tendency of the theology, that I venture to describe as the leading theology of our days, I will characterize by the words realistic and radical. These two words then may be considered as complementary. They are aiming at the same goal. They are expressing a common tendency with different but complementary shades. As derived from *radix* and taken in its original sense the word radical will, just as strongly as the word realistic, indicate the necessity to see Christianity *as it is*, according to its own origin and originality. Throughout the ages Christianity has been interpreted in many different ways. No interpretation can pretend not to be influenced by its own time and spiritual situation. Nevertheless, Christianity has by no means that chameleon-like quality of changing at pleasure, and it certainly must be the chief task of theology to liberate Christianity as much as possible from all over-paintings hiding its fresh colors and thus to let its religious motives appear in all their original power. The realism here aimed at is nothing but the realism of Christianity itself. The intention is that the Christian revelation, its views of God, of Christ, of Church, of man, of Christian life, of evil, of history and of the world may appear just as they are. The radical view means that the Christian motives are not to be blunted or weakened in one way or another, that God's *agape* may be explained in all its fullness and that God's claim on man may be maintained without any compromises.

A realistic and radical interpretation of Christianity must then indubitably repudiate certain ideas belonging to traditional pietism as well as to modernism. It will, for instance, in traditional pietism find a tendency to idealize the Christian life and at the same time to paint an unmodulated black picture of the world. On the other side, modernism cannot be acquitted from gilding the human life and at the same time from impoverishing the richness of the Christian message. But such objections don't mean that the movements in question ought to be considered only as a parenthesis in the history of Christianity. There are tendencies in pietism as well as in modernism that ought never to be overlooked. The pietistic emphasis upon personal piety must never be forgotten. But also the tendency of modernism to find positive relations to contemporary culture must be maintained. The fault of modernism was not that it represented such a tendency. The fault was rather that its interpretation was no true translation, but instead of that a remoulding transformation of the Christian message.

As regards the change in the theological outlook here indicated, two factors have had a dominating influence: firstly, a new and deeper insight into the intentions of the Reformation; secondly, a new, fresh and realistic approach to the biblical message. The first forward move came from the Reformation. In different Churches and in different ways, theology turned back to the living well-springs of the Reformation. The Reformation was seen not as it had stiffened in the formulas of the old orthodoxy, or as it had been re-interpreted in the theological schools of the later centuries, but instead of that the religious motives of the Reformation were sought out. And it proved that these motives were at the same time active forces that set theology in motion and led it along towards a regeneration.

It is, however, only reasonable that this theological movement could not make a halt at the Reformation. The reformers did not, as is well known, wish to preach a new Gospel or to build a new Church, they wanted only to reveal the Gospel of the Bible. Therefore, nothing can be more natural than the fact that the deeper penetration of the motives of the Reformation led directly forward to intensified biblical studies. One of the most striking features of the present theological situation is indubitably the revolution that has taken place in exegetic research. This revolution did not at all mean a return to a tradition-tied, legalistic and doctrinal fundamentalism, and abandonment of the critical investigation of the Bible, but it meant a new interest in and a new concentration upon the characteristic and central message of the Bible. At the same time the Bible was no more, as in the earlier research, judged and criticized from "modern" lines of thought, unfamiliar to the Bible itself, and therefore leading to a remoulding interpretation of the biblical message. The aim of the investigation was primarily to read and understand the Bible from its own points of view. The result was a discovery of the unity that existed in the Bible in spite of all variations, a discovery of its central and unitary message.

Theology marching towards a realistic and radical interpretation of Christianity has not arrived at its goal. Certainly, it has not finished its work. It is rather a theology in process of formation. That being the case it is only quite natural that it appears in various forms, and that its representatives often hold different and even opposing views. But behind all the differences, you will find a very definite and conscious endeavor to reach and maintain the authenticity of Christianity and to find a firm biblical anchorage for these endeavors.

It is not my intention to give a survey of the theological situation in different parts of the world. But nobody will, I hope, disapprove if I should now try quite briefly to illustrate the theological movement in question as seen from a Swedish horizon, just as I myself have witnessed it during nearly fifty years as a theological student. I am not so pretentious that I will describe this Swedish theology as ideal or prefigurative. But in all humbleness I think that the Swedish theology—among many other theologies—has made a contribution to a realistic and radical interpretation of Christianity. The starting-point of the new orientation in my country came at the beginning of this century, when Nathan Söderblom with his comprehensive perspectives liberated the Swedish theology from isolation or from one-sided dependence upon German theology, and when Einar Billing found new impulses through fresh studies of Luther. It is not possible to describe here the important contributions of these two pioneers, nor to give an account of the following development. I must confine myself to emphasizing four points as characteristic of the changed orientation.

1. The first point concerns the chief motive of the Reformation, its vindication of salvation as the free and quite undeserved gift of God's grace, of his *agape*. The new and fresh confrontation with Luther quite naturally opened the eyes for the whole radicalism of this message about God's way to and acceptance of sinful man. The center of this message being God's *agape*, "justification by faith alone" means quite the same as "justification by God's *agape* alone." Faith is no subjective quality and still less a human merit. Faith means on the contrary that our eyes are turned away from ourselves and from all subjective considerations to the objective fact of God's *agape* as acting with us in and through Christ. According to Luther's expressive words, faith *"rapit nos a nobis et ponit nos extra nos."* Faith "snatches us away from ourselves and puts us outside ourselves." Thus we don't build on our own, on our deeds or experiences, but only on God's redeeming *agape*, the actions of which, being spontaneous, free and overflowing, don't depend on any values of its object. When this divine Love reveals itself in Christ, sacrificing itself, it at the same time reveals its highest majesty.

The difference between this view and the humanizing theology of modernism is obvious. Here is no place for a moralizing interpretation, nor for an idealization of man. Salvation is not a strengthening of "the divine part" of man, but a salvation of man as a whole. But there are also remarkable differences in relation to the traditional pietistic view. One of them appears very clearly in the conception of man as redeemed. In his book *The Nature and Destiny of Man* Reinhold Niebuhr very correctly writes about the Reformation: "it was the historical locus where the Christian conscience became most fully aware of the persistence of sin in the life of the redeemed." One of the most significant formulas of Luther was that the redeemed man is *simul iustus et peccator,* at the same time righteous and a sinner. I will not try here to analyze this comprehensive formula in detail. It may be enough to say that this conception stands up against all tendencies towards a perfectionist interpretation and that it means the most uncompromising and realistic view of the Christian life.

2. The second point has reference to the conception of history as drama. The perfectionist interpretation of history is rejected just as is the perfectionist interpretation of the Christian life. History is not an evolution towards a perfection within the boundaries of this world and this time. But on the other hand it is far from meaningless. It has the deepest meaning, because it is a drama where God's *agape* fights against the evil forces opposed to the will of God. The Christian idea of salvation stands out against this background. Therefore, revelation cannot be understood only from the intellectual point of view. For it is not a doctrine, it is an action, God's action in history. From this point of view

we must see the life and work of Christ, His message, His sacrifice and His victory. Certainly, His Kingdom "is not of this world." The evolutionary view is replaced by the eschatological. But that does not mean that eschatology would be a metaphysical idea and that God's Kingdom would have nothing to do with the present world. The work of Christ "is finished" (John 19:30), but at the same time it is continued for all time and for all generations. The Kingdom is, as long as time lasts, a fighting Kingdom where Christ now, as in His earthly days, fights His enemies. And here His words in St. Luke 11:20 are applicable: "If I with the finger of God cast out devils, no doubt the kingdom of God is come upon you."

3. The third point is a rediscovery of the Church, a new consciousness of her essence and her central importance for the Christian life. This rediscovery was immediately connected with the Christian message just described. Christ continues His work in and through His Church. Then Church, then, is an expression of the spontaneous and universally directed divine *agape*, the *gratia preveniens*, and so she is a living witness for the always active divine revelation. As such, the Church, the actual Church of history, is the mother of every Christian. Therefore, the Church is seen from an organic and dynamic point of view: the Church reaches as far as the divine *agape* in Christ is working in human hearts. This view obviously differs from the modernist as well as the pietistic attitude towards the Church. Modernism had a very small interest in the Church. It considered her rather as an aberration from

the original doctrine of Jesus. The traditional pietistic conception was individualistic as far as it saw the individual as primary in relation to the church-fellowship, and apprehended the Church as a kind of union of individual Christians with the same or at least similar experiences.

This new estimation of the Church was by no means an attempt to idealize the Church. The idea was not to conceal the infirmities and sins of the actual Church of history. On the contrary, the mistakes and sins appeared much clearer than ever when the Church was seen in this light. But at the same time, because the divine power, Christ and His Spirit are working in all human weaknesses, the actual Church of history is, in spite of all, something more than only a frail human society—she is the body of Christ and the instrument of His fighting Kingdom.

Before dealing with my fourth point I should now like to say some few words about the biblical investigations in recent times that have had so great an importance everywhere in Christendom, and also for our Swedish theology. The subject is very comprehensive, and I must confine myself to two remarks, the first about the biblical message as a whole, and the second about the idea of the Church in the New Testament.

In the time before historical criticism, the scholastic period, the Bible was considered as a unity without varieties, all the contents of the Bible being conceived as on the same level, the infallible divine word. The result of the earlier historical criticism very often seemed to be varieties without unity. Indeed, the Bible even seemed to be split up not only in varieties but also in seemingly irreconcilable contradictions. The stage that the investigations have reached in recent times could be characterized as unity in varieties. Certainly the present theology has as keen an eye as before for the varieties in the Bible. Nevertheless, the unity of the Christian message is strongly emphasized. The *kerygma* of the New Testament is quite definite and is substantially the same in the gospels and in the apostolic epistles. In spite of all varieties, the New Testament stands out as an extraordinarily firm unity with Christos-Kyrios as its center.

From this center new light is thrown upon the idea and reality of the Church. Christ and the Church belong together. They cannot be separated from each other. Obviously the time has passed when the idea of the Church in the New Testament could be disregarded as of only secondary importance, and when it could be interpreted from an individualistic point of view. Christianity appeared as the Church. To be a Christian is, according to the New Testament, to be a member of the Church, to have a share in the new *koinonia*, the new communion that was "the body of Christ." This phrase, the body of Christ, is not to be understood only as figurative. The body of Christ is for the New Testament a concrete, living reality. The living Christ is in a very real and concrete way working in His Church through His Word and His sacraments. The Church is a revelation of the invisible Lord, a continued incarnation of Christ on earth. He is Himself the head of the Church, the source from which the power is derived that leads, governs and holds the whole together, fighting the sins and the infirmities that the New Testament certainly does not conceal. As the Church of Christ, the Church is a heavenly organism, but at the same time perceptible and visible on earth, existing on the border between two worlds, two aeons, having a quality that transcends every present age of history.

It is not, of course, my intention to say that the biblical investigations have led to a unanimous interpretation of Christianity. Far from that! Nevertheless, the new and intense approach to the witness of the Bible means not only an endeavor towards a deeper and more realistic interpretation of the Christian message, but also new possibilities of an increasing communion in the world of theology and of the Churches. The tendencies, for instance, of a Lutheran theology to stop at Luther or of a reformed theology to stop at Calvin, that in old times have been so outstanding, cannot but be eliminated.

After this excursion to biblical witness, I now return to my fourth point. It concerns the universal perspective of Christianity.

When you read what I have said about the first three points, you probably got an impression of a theology that at least tried sincerely to explain Christianity in its own unique individuality. You may not raise any objections to such a theological purpose. You may even approve that it must be the primary task of theology to explain the true character of Christianity. But at the same time you will perhaps ask if such an interpretation, that could be described as Theocentric, Christocentric and also Church-centric, will not lead to an exclusiveness, which isolates Christianity and shuts it up in its own more or less confined world. In fact, it would be easily understandable if you should raise such a question, because it cannot be denied that a purifying work of theology has sometimes also been an isolating work.

On the other hand, it is obvious that theology, trying to establish positive relations to culture and society, has often embarked upon very risky ways. It was a risky way when theology in old times used to speak about a natural religion and a natural theology, and it was no less risky when theology in recent times practiced idolatry with the so-called orders of creation and then, for instance, landed in an idolization of the actual state. Evidently it cannot be advisable to establish contact with culture and society at the sacrifice of the true character of Christianity. But such a line of action is not indeed necessary. On the contrary, a position of exclusiveness and isolation is indubitably a sign that the religious perspective has been reduced and blunted. As regards these questions, the decisive fact is that we really understand what it means that God is the living God of all the universe. According to the Christian message Christ is the only way to salvation. But that does not mean that all the work of God should be confined to Christ. God does not work only through His Gospel, only through Christ and His Church; He works also through His Law, the Universal Law of the Creator. When He is acting in history, fighting His enemies by Law and judgment, creating order out of chaos, justice out of unrighteousness, then He also uses as His instruments men who don't belong to His Church. The root of the false exclusiveness is not the message of salvation through Christ, that also is a universal message; instead of that, it is a view that considers the world only as profane, forgetting that the world, in spite of all evil and sin, in spite of all satanic forces, is nevertheless the world of God, and His laboratory. Without this religious and Christian perspective, you will never be able to see the problems of history, of Christianity and of Society from a true Christian aspect—your interpretation of Christianity will lead either to isolation or to false pretensions from the side of the Christians. Your interpretation will lack the necessary realism and radicalism.

II

THE WORLD CRISIS AND THE CHURCH

THE world-catastrophe that our generation has lived through was not only a material devastation such as the world formerly never has seen. It was at the same time a moral catastrophe. We witnessed the most disastrous dethronement of justice. The policy of brute force·violated even the most elementary claims of justice in a way that we never thought to be possible. Aggression had no moral limitations. It was carried through just as far as power permitted. That which happened in our midst, in the heart of Europe, was in any case a setting aside of all that we, not only from a Christian but also from a human point of view, acknowledge as justice and righteousness. With horror we were looking into the grimacing face of a demoniacal state of amorality.

Indeed, mankind ought to have been utterly hardened through the events of history. Throughout the life of mankind we find in abundance wars, terrors, atrocities, blood and tears. Persecutions, massacres and sadism are not unknown in history. In the French as well as in the Russian revolutions torrents of blood have been shed. Both these revolutions began with open hostility against Christianity and the Church. A persecution of the Church like that of the first years of the Soviet-rule, the Church has not suffered since the great persecutions of the old Roman Empire. Nevertheless the national-socialist regime in Germany holds a unique position, in that here the self-glorious state without morality and conscience was brought to ripeness. Everybody could see what was and must be the result when justice was brushed aside or—what in fact was the same thing—was transformed to a slave of the will to power. The terrible atrocities and the sadistic brutalities were not accidental, they belonged to the system. They were consequences of the "principles" that were vindicated and systematically realized without any restraint.

Machiavelli is considered as the man who in his famous book *Il Principe* first asserted that the government of a state must be free from all moral obligations. He did not say that the state ought never to speak in the name of morality. If that proved to suit its purpose, the state ought to use moral arguments. But then, of course, the moral is nothing but camouflage. According to Machiavelli no other principles for the government could be approved except the principles of might and self-assertion. Such thoughts were of course not new, still less were actions of that kind unknown. Nevertheless, it really was a novelty that such an amorality was acknowledged as the leading principle for the conduct of the state, and that the basic principles for which Christianity had fought through centuries were dismissed. There was no other law for the state than its own "law," and this law could only be the self-assertion of unlimited power that would go as far as its resources allowed. What the Middle Ages had described as a tyrant, Machiavelli described as the ideal sovereign. Our own time has had the first and very doubtful honor of realizing more consistently and more ruthlessly than ever before the program of Machiavelli. The leader of the national-socialism permitted himself to do all those things that Machiavelli permitted his sovereign—and even more, to throw all moral considerations to the wind. In fact, Machiavelli got more than he bargained for.

Now, if we had told the national-socialist regime that it had brushed aside all justice, certainly it would not have accepted our criticism. The Nazis would not grant that they had left all the claims of justice behind them. They would rather tell us that we had our kind of justice and that they themselves had quite another kind of justice, the justice of blood and soil, the justice that belonged to the master-people. From that point of view they would criticize us, maintaining that our view of law and justice was far too weak and feeble, far too much influenced by humanitarian and Christian points of view. If then we had tried to discuss these questions with them, rational arguments would not have been of much use. Our antagonists would not have listened. We should not have found that common ground that is necessary for a fruitful discussion. Our antagonists would only have told us that our view of law and justice rested on assumptions that they could not accept.

But even if we must, therefore, despair of our possibilities to convince them, we have every reason to make clear why *we* cannot accept their view. Trying to make that clear, we are at the same time confronted with the question of what really constitutes and is essential for a justice that can be accepted as justice.

Two reasons make it quite impossible for us to accept the view of law and justice as shown by the national-socialist conception. The first is that their "justice" is only a very limited justice. It is only a particular, not a universal justice. What here is called justice is only valid for certain privileged peoples, races and persons. It is a privilege for the master-people, but it is not valid for other peoples and races. They are excluded from this so-called justice. They have no legal security, no legal rights. What is right for the Aryans is not right for other races, for instance for the Jews. The Nordic blood decides what is right and what is not, what ought and what ought not to be done. That means that the most elementary claim of justice has been trampled to death, the claim namely that justice must be the same for all. A justice that is a privilege for certain persons or classes, or peoples or races, and therefore is not valid for all, is no longer justice.

The second reason for our rejection of the so-called justice of the national-socialism is nearly connected with the first. It is that justice here loses its majesty. Justice is being degraded to an element which the momentary power of the state uses just as it likes, quite arbitrarily and without all restraint. Obviously this view leads to a denial not only of the commandment that we ought to love our neighbor as ourselves, but also of all that humanity stands for. Humanitarian aspects and considerations are and must be regarded as weakness and a leniency that only spoiled the sense of glory and pride that belonged to the master-race and that at any price must be safeguarded. Altogether, the national-socialist ideology was characterized by indifference and contempt for the individual. In relation to the state and race he had no rights. According to the prevailing conception of justice, crimes were never committed against individuals, only against state, people and race. As regards the supremacy of might over right, the Nazi regime was very outspoken. It proclaimed that justice was incarnated in the leader and that the Führer himself in his plenitude of power had to decide what was right and what was not. Justice did not by any means stand above the power of the state. Instead of that it was a servant that the momentary might of the state used just as it liked for enforcing its will. Justice had thus been completely relativized. It had lost its sovereignty.

Our criticism has led to two fundamental statements about justice. Justice must be universal: it must be a justice for all. And justice must be sovereign: it cannot be transformed into a flunky for the government in function. A state, especially a modern state, has plenty of tasks. But the most fundamental task must be by way of the Law to preserve the order of justice and righteousness. Then it is an indispensable condition that justice is considered as something more than only a slave of the state. Certainly, justice as order cannot be preserved and maintained without help from the power of the state. The situation is not such that we should have to choose only between might and right. In fact, we cannot have right as a judicial system without might. But that does not mean that right is identical with organized power, as it sometimes has been pretended. In fact, we often find a fighting antagonism between right and might, and the cause of justice vindicated against a superior power. The consciousness of right and justice frequently offers resistance against an order that a physical power will realize. Indeed, justice can very well be maintained even without the means of might, even under persecutions and sufferings. Considering these facts, we must state that while justice in order to be realized is more or less dependent on the power of a state or of a union of states, nevertheless, it is also in itself a power, and even a power that cannot be destroyed through violation. If a state is to be a state of justice, the condition is that the majesty of justice is recognized. Justice must be held in respect and honor. The power of the state must, for instance, run the risk that it can be the losing side in a judicial controversy settled by a court of law. At the very instant when a state considers justice as a servant whom it can command and use as it likes, this state has ceased to be a state of justice. Then it has fallen among thieves and has surrendered itself to the demon of power.

Before the complete breakdown of justice that our generation has witnessed we must inevitably ask ourselves: how was it possible that something like that

on the whole could happen? Many books have already
been written on that subject. I will not claim to be
able to explain all the different reasons that led to this
manifestation of evil powers which here unmasked
themselves in all their horribleness. Indubitably there
are many facts in the history of Germany, in the older
as well as especially in the more recent, that have laid
the foundation for the coming of national-socialism.
Many prominent names could be mentioned as well
from political as from philosophical and literary
spheres. Strong movements among the people of ex-
treme nationalism and a remarkable will to obey "leaders" can also be brought forward as helping to solve
the riddle which, in spite of all explanations, will con-
tinue to be a riddle.

Nevertheless, it would be self-righteousness and
hypocrisy for us to pretend that the tendencies that
led to such a breakdown of justice were only to be
found in Germany. It would be just as absurd as to
pretend that the world-crisis had passed, and that the
problem of justice was solved merely by the victory
over the Nazi regime.

It is obvious that for a long time we have witnessed
a continual weakening and a process of disintegration
of the consciousness of justice. Two questions here are
of great importance. One has reference to what has
happened in the secularized world. The other question
concerns the attitude of the Churches. We must ask
how far the Churches have acted according to their
duty and responsibility towards Society. Many reproaches have been addressed to the Churches, not least

to the Churches that are associated with the Lutheran Reformation. We have every reason seriously to consider such reproaches as well as the attitude of the Churches on the whole. Indeed, a self-examination of the Church is inevitable and most important. It would be very objectionable if, for instance, the Churches should try to acquit themselves by throwing all the blame for the development on the secularized world. Therefore, in this book accent will be laid upon the question of the attitude of the Church and her self-examination.

As regards the relativization of the idea of justice in and through the secularization I will confine myself to some short remarks. As has just been suggested the relativization of the idea of justice has been going on for a long time. The process of the dissolution was for some time concealed through the thought, based upon the idea of *lex naturae,* that justice was a metaphysical element that had authority in itself. When this metaphysical aspect by and by disappeared through critical analysis, justice could not but lose its supreme authority, and finally nothing was left but only the different human interests struggling for their different "rights." Then justice had been completely relativized. The question of justice was degraded to a question of having power enough to realize the "rights" that an individual or a class or a state pretended to possess. Man was no longer subordinated to any claims regarded as inviolable, unshakable and holy. Might then had taken precedence over justice and right.

For the moment we will leave the question about

the responsibility of the Church. Later we will return
to it, trying to examine if and how the Church—naturally enough against her own will—may have co-operated in the dissolution of the idea of justice. However, it cannot be denied that such a dissolution has
taken place, nor that it has been at least a contributing
circumstance to the world crisis. Only we must not
forget that the tendencies leading to the dethronement
of the idea of justice have been working everywhere
in our civilization. The self-glorious state without moral
considerations was brought to ripeness in the Nazi
regime. But the great danger is that such tendencies
are to be found everywhere, concealing themselves behind different screens. The self-gloriousness of the state
appears in various disguises. There are totalitarian
ideologies and masks, but there are also democratic
masks. The chief thing then must be to unveil the
amorality that conceals itself behind the different
masks.

However, our description of the present situation
would be one-sided and therefore wrong, if we should
speak only about the bankruptcy of justice. Indeed,
we have witnessed not only the offense against justice
and its breakdown, but we have also witnessed how
the wounded and violated sense of justice and righteousness has risen and offered resistance. The dreadful
events of course provoked horror and indignation. They
also provoked hate. The reactions and feelings may
have been miscellaneous and in addition influenced by
strong political propaganda. Nevertheless, it would be
a complete misunderstanding and misjudging of the

situation, if we should underestimate the very important role played by the challenged sense of righteousness. That does not mean that the war was considered as a crusade. Thought of that kind belonged perhaps to the first world war. As regards the second world war, the Nazis, as is well remembered, tried to propagate their fight against Soviet Russia as a crusade. From the other side the war was not spoken of as a crusade. Here it was in a very realistic way considered rather as a dirty job that ought to be done because a regime such as that combated necessarily must make it quite impossible for the nations to live tolerably together on earth. But already this point of view shows clearly the activity of the violated sense of justice. And on the whole, the moral resistance undoubtedly has been a very important factor in the gigantic fight that led to victory. It has to a great extent given this fight its inner strength and has so had an importance in the realm of high politics.

We have every reason to emphasize this fact. It tells us that a policy, going on without any moral considerations, has no right to call itself a realistic policy. It tells us that moral factors and rules are realities to be taken into consideration. In spite of all, there are moral rules that we cannot let go unpunished. The policy of the cynical type likes claiming to be "realistic." But it is not. A policy that is in truth realistic must take into account not only might and violence, not only economic factors, but also moral principles which are essential for the living together of humanity.

The world crisis with all its dissolutions of justice

and righteousness meant a very hard trial also for the Churches. Now the question of the Church's relation to Society was more than ever actualized. It was brought to the most acute stage. How, then, did the Churches react in this situation? And how did they explain and justify their actions? It is very important for us to find an answer to these questions. The attitude of the Churches in the hard crisis will help us to see more clearly what the responsibility of the Church towards Society really implies.

I have just spoken about the spontaneous resistance against the violation of justice. First, we must observe and accent that this resistance had a very broad basis. Quite naturally it was strong in the Churches. But it was by no means confined only to Christian circles and unions. The defense of the principle of righteousness was no Christian monopoly. The resistance appeared, strongly and intensely, also in circles that were more or less strangers to Christianity and belonged to secularized humanity. No religious boundaries prevented the co-operation between men who otherwise belonged to different camps. Christians and secularized persons united in a common struggle. They all felt themselves challenged to defend the distressed cause of humanity. They saw with new clearness that the maintenance of the order of justice is the foundation as much of life in a particular state as of international life.

As regards the Churches, the shocking experiences could not but awake their responsibility. They could not stand aside. They felt themselves forced to act, and they did act—just as Churches. Even if their position was not always irreproachable, even if there existed traitors among their servants, and even if other servants did not clearly understand what was going on, we certainly can state that the Churches on a large scale deeply felt their responsibility, and that they were centers for the opposition against violation and for the strengthening of the sense of justice and righteousness in the different fighting countries.

It is necessary first to say some words about the situation in Germany itself. After the national-socialists' entry into the possession of power, the conflict between Church and State immediately started. The Nazis did not openly declare their hostility against religion and the Church. They concealed their heathenism and their moral nihilism behind phrases about a so-called positive Christianity. I shall never forget a discussion that I had in Denmark in 1934 with a German Nazi jurist. He tried to inform me that the Nazi rule would not at all attack Christianity. Then he added these words: *nur nichts gegen die nationale Weltanschauung*—only nothing against the nationalist conception of life. This statement speaks for itself. In fact, it tells us all about the real position of the national-socialists. Christianity and Church could be tolerated just as long as they accepted and bowed to the Nazi ideology, that was highest authority. The theory was that the Church had only to do with other-worldiness, and was not allowed to interfere in temporal questions.

Now it is well known that there existed in Germany many churchmen as well among the Roman Catholics as, perhaps even more, among the Protestants who compromised with the Nazis and even, more or less, accepted their theories of blood and race, thus betraying the cause of Christianity. Others tried to work as usual without taking any definite position. For Lutherdom it is a great sorrow that some Lutheran theologians tried to defend their self-effacement before the totalitarian state through, as I will demonstrate later, a wrong interpretation of Luther, and by so doing disgraced the reformer.

But after having spoken about these treasons we must emphasize the fact that in both the great confessions there existed a strong and intense opposition against the Nazis and their methods. The struggle was, from the Churches' side, fought under most difficult circumstances and most dreadful risks. The position of the Protestants was even more difficult than the position of the Roman Catholics, partly because the Protestants were divided into different Church organizations, partly because these Churches, since the Reformation, had been state Churches and therefore were more dependent on the state. They were not supported by a world-wide Church organization such as the Roman. They must fight alone, while the Roman Catholics were strengthened for instance by the very outspoken encyclical of Pope Pius XI of 1937 to the German bishops. It ought to be observed that the struggle of both the confessions in the first place was a fight for the freedom of the Church against the oppression of the Nazi rule, a struggle for the life of the Church. However, when the Nazi rule more and more realized its policy of terror, and especially after the atrocities against the

Jewish race, the Churches also began by and by to denounce the violence of law and justice.

When the German military forces occupied most of the countries in Europe and when the Nazi-commissioners, partly with help of some native traitors, terrorized the occupied peoples in the most dreadful way, quite despising all international agreements, the Churches everywhere felt themselves obliged to speak on behalf of violated justice. The audacity of the Churches may have varied in the different countries. Nevertheless, it must undoubtedly be said that the Churches on the whole, in the time of trial, carefully made use of their possibilities as defenders of righteousness and its claims.

We find an excellent and elucidating illustration of the behavior of the Church in the actions and statements of the Norwegian Church during the occupation of Norway. Some characteristic features may here be mentioned. In January, 1941, the bishops of the Norwegian Church delivered a statement to one of the "Ministers" in the cabinet of the notorious traitor Quisling. In this statement they very strongly opposed the violations of justice that had just taken place in Norway. The points of the accusations were three. The government in exercising its function had violated the courts of law, and had thus forced the Supreme Court of Juridicature to resign. Further, the youth organization of the national-socialists in Norway (the so-called *hird*, the body of housecarls) was allowed to undertake undue aggressions without being punished. Finally, the government in exercising its function was interfer-

THE WORLD CRISIS AND THE CHURCH

ing with the right of the clergy to keep secrets given under the seal of the confession. All of which meant, said the bishops, that the Norwegian law had ceased to function and that a status of anarchy prevailed in the country. The government was seriously admonished in accordance with its duty to reorganize and maintain the judicial system.

During a personal interview with the "minister" some weeks later, the bishops very clearly justified their action. They maintained that it is useless to try to dismiss the Church by saying that she is mixing into politics. They quoted some words of Luther: "The Church is not interfering in worldly affairs when she exhorts the authorities to be obedient to the highest authority, which is God." I will cite some more words from the statement of the bishops. "When the leaders of the community permit violence and practice injustice and coerce the soul, then the Church is the guardian of the soul.—With all its human weakness the Church is authorized by God to teach His Law and His Gospel to all people. Therefore, the Church can never remain silent where God's word is ignored and where sin arises. In this the Church is adamant and cannot in these essentials be bound by any government. We therefore exhort the heads of the community to end all which conflicts with God's holy arrangements regarding justice, truth, freedom of conscience and goodness, and to build entirely on God's Law of living."

This statement opened the long and hard fight between the Norwegian Church and the Nazi rule in Norway. When looking back at the three points it is

obvious that the matter of contention wholly concerned
the question of justice. That is applicable even to the
third point. Certainly this point at a cursory glance
concerns the freedom of the Church. But on closer
examination we see that the Church even here acted
on behalf of justice. In fact, the Nazi-rule wanted to
force the Church to reveal the secrets given under the
seal of the confession, thus to be able to judge the
persons in question by the Nazi courts.

When next time the Church opposed the Nazi government, she again acted on behalf of justice and
righteousness. The bishops vehemently denounced a
law, given by Quisling, that stated that all the Norwegian youth should be educated in accordance with
the prototype of the so-called Hitler-youth in Germany.
The bishops declared that such a law was contradictory
to the Norwegian law as well as to the commandments
of God.

Now, of course the fight of the Norwegian Church
also developed into a very hard struggle for the freedom of the Church. The maintenance of justice and
freedom for the Church was the aim for the fight
throughout the years of the occupation. In emphasizing
how from the very beginning the fight was against
the violation of justice, my intention is to show how
deeply the Church here felt her responsibility. As
regards the motives for the action of the Church
we must observe two things. The Church derived
her arguments from the existing law of the land as
well as from international law. But the deepest reason for her actions was to be found in her responsibility

before the Law of God. The Church, being entrusted with the word of God, could, as the bishops said, not be silent when the most elementary commandments of God were violated. She would have failed in her duty if she had not spoken. Secondly, as regards the aforementioned misinterpretation of Luther by some German theologians it may not be unimportant to point out that the Norwegian Churchmen found support in Luther and often referred to statements in which he said that it was the duty of the Church to "admonish the consciences" when the secular power failed to fulfill its duties and performed the deeds of the devil instead of the works of God according to His Law.

The action of the Church of Norway is a characteristic illustration of the fight between Church and State during the world war. Even though all the Churches did not everywhere and consistently hold quite the same strong position as the Norwegian Church, nevertheless the situation was a similar one in all the occupied countries. Everywhere the fight was not only a fight for the freedom of the Church, but also a fight for justice and righteousness.

Considering this attitude of the Churches in the terrible world crisis, two points ought to be emphasized. The first is that the Church, feeling her responsibility toward Society, justified her actions by referring in some way or other to the Law that the Church had to guard and at the same time serve as the armory from which the weapons were fetched. A certain difference can be proved as regards the argumentation. While the Protestants referred directly to the Law of

God, the Roman Catholics liked to refer to "the natural Law." The second point is that the defense of the principles of justice was not at all confined to confessing Christians. The dividing line did not go between confessing Christians and a secularized society, but between those who did and those who did not consider the principle of justice and righteousness as a holy duty, never to be betrayed and deserted.

The great tragedy that our generation has witnessed must be seen against the background of a long decline of the sense of righteousness. The most important question from the point of view of the Church is now whether the Church herself is implicated in this decline. Has the Church in any way co-operated in this deplorable development? Here we must not think only upon the neglects and mistakes of the Church in her relation to Society. It is obvious that there exists plenty of such neglects and mistakes in the history of the Church. Yet our examination must penetrate deeper. It must try to discover whether motives in the failure of the Church are to be found in dominating interpretations of Christianity and views of the Church, and in the conceptions of the purpose of the Church. Our analysis then must be a self-examination of the Church.

III

SELF-EXAMINATION OF
THE CHURCH

THE relation of the Church and Society has been exposed to two main temptations. The first is a temptation to passivity and indifference, the second to false pretensions and to embracing Utopian and illusionary ideals. Both these temptations can meet and have in fact met in various guises. It is useless to say that it has not been only a question of temptations. Undoubtedly the Church often has yielded to them. Then through her passivity she has promoted not only the secularization but also the decline of the sense of righteousness. And through her false pretensions and Utopian ideas she has more or less spoiled her possibilities to strengthen the cause of justice.

Plenty of accusations also have been raised against the attitude of the Church, not least in the last centuries. They have referred to the passivity as well as to the activity of the Church. It has been said that the Church has done far too little for social and international life, and also that she pretends too much and that she assumes an exclusiveness, a monopoly that cannot be justified. The accusations therefore some-

times may contradict each other. Nevertheless there
can exist good reasons in both cases. A Church that
is not afraid of a thorough self-examination has every
reason for listening to and seriously considering the
charges against her behavior.

The first category of charges tells us that the Church,
on a large scale, has been indifferent to the great social
and international problems. She has retired far too
much into her own shell and left the "world" out of
consideration. But a position of indifference is very
easily transformed to a position of reactionary resistance. That means that the Church has acted very often
as a restraining force which has put obstacles in the
way of necessary reforms. The great reforms then have
been realized not with the help of the Church but in
spite of her resistance. From this point of view we
have to understand the well-known catchword that the
Church is "opiate for the people." The Church has been
too feeble and lenient towards those in possession of
power. She also has shown tendencies to kneel before
the nationalist state, her attitude being characterized
by yieldingness and self-effacement.

Now nobody can deny that there are reasons for all
these charges. On the other side it is obvious that the
reproaches in question do not tell us the whole truth
about the attitude of the Church. It is not my intention to examine when and how far the Church has
failed through passivity and feebleness. But there is
another question that must come up for discussion, the
question namely whether the blameful attitude of the
Church has its roots in Christianity itself and there-

fore must be considered as a consequence of the Christian position. The accusations here mainly have paid attention to two Christian lines of thought, first to the other-worldliness of Christianity, then to the Christian conception of man and history. It is said that the other-worldliness of Christianity necessarily turns men's eyes away from this earth and its problems, considering the life in this world as something less essential. Further, the conception of man emphasizes the sinfulness of humanity and states with St. John that all the world lies in the power of evil. The conclusion is that such lines of thought must subdue and even kill the activity of man for creating a better society.

The second category of charges attacks the activity of the Church or perhaps rather the self-overestimation that can appear in Christian quarters when the relationship between Church and Society is discussed. It is said that the Church sometimes speaks as if she alone were able to stand for justice and righteousness and as though Christianity were considered the only foundation of righteousness without which justice could never be held sacred. This line of thought can also take another and more personal course. It can be maintained that the problems of Society can be solved only through men seriously Christianized. Such a change in the souls of men is thought as the decisive and only possible condition for establishing a new and better state of things in the life of Society. It would at the same time mean that the Kingdom of God was on the road to being realized in the world. When theories of this kind are rejected as pre-

sumptuous and supercilious, for instance from a secularized humanity, it can at the same time be maintained
that the theories have their anchorage in Christianity,
that they are connected with the outlook upon the
Christian life which alleges that man cannot do anything good without being converted.

An investigation as to what has been said about the
temptations and accusations must distinguish between
two questions. One concerns the reality behind the reproaches. For giving a full answer it would be necessary to write a complete history of the Church from
the beginning up to our own days. As we have already
admitted, there have often but not always existed good
reasons for the charges. Quite another is the question
that we must now try to answer, namely the question
whether the failures of the Church, as far as they exist,
have their origin in Christianity itself or rather whether
they are based upon one-sided and misleading interpretations. From this point of view we will now first examine the meaning of the other-worldiness of Christianity and its conception of man and history.

Indubitably the other-worldiness is an integral element of Christianity. "My Kingdom is not from hence."
The outlook of Christianity is towards "the world to
come." Not at least in recent times theology, as is well
known, has strongly accentuated the eschatological
view of Christianity and of the Kingdom of God. Opposing earlier tendencies to apprehend the Kingdom
of God from an immanent point of view, it was stated
that such an optimistic and more or less evolutionary
conception was quite strange to the New Testament.

Indubitably this criticism was quite justified. It cannot be denied that the conception of the Bible is decidedly eschatological and strongly emphasizes the other-worldliness of the Kingdom. Therefore, a belief in a progressive development within the world would be to leave the Bible out of consideration. According to the Bible, the world cannot be changed into the Kingdom of God. The world always remains "world." The realization and fulfillment of the Kingdom of God do not belong to the present age, but to the age to come. However, quite another question is, in fact, whether this view must lead the Church to an indifferent and negative attitude towards "the world," towards Society and its problems. If that is so, the Church would live as a stranger and outsider in the world of history. The Church would live her own life within her own fixed boundaries, and all that happened outside these boundaries would be no concern of the Church. Now it is a curious fact, well certified in recent times, that such a conception of the Church's purpose and life is very agreeable to and eagerly maintained by politicians who want to fetter the Church and cut her freedom short so as unrestrainedly to realize their own power-politics. From this quarter it is again and again said that the Church's domain is "the other-worldliness" and that she must keep clear of all that belongs to this world and the dominions of the state. Face to face with such doctrines unfolded by the oppressors of the Church we must be more than suspicious. It does not seem very likely that the Church and her oppressors could hold the same opinions as regards the purpose and work of the Church.

Without reserve it must of course be admitted that the eschatological view of the Realm of God sometimes has been used as a motive for a more or less indifferent attitude towards Society and History. However, conclusions in such a direction are based upon a one-sided interpretation that leaves very important elements of the biblical view out of sight. No objection can be raised to the eschatological view as such. It certainly is essential. The other-worldiness of the Realm of God must not be softened or concealed. But the eschatological view of the Bible does not mean a transcendence from which history disappears as unessential. On the contrary, the Kingdom has a very close relation to history, and eschatology means also a definite view of history. It means not to flee from history, but to see history from the aspect of the Realm of God. Christ says that His Kingdom "is not from hence," but at the same time He asks His disciples to pray that the will of God be done in earth as it is in heaven. We must never forget that the New Testament looks upon history as a drama where the battle between God and the dark, hostile forces of evil is unceasingly being fought. This fight makes history a meaningful process. In fact, nothing can possibly give a deeper meaning to history.

In the fight for the Realm of God the decisive victory has been won by Christ. That means a breaking-through of a new aeon, the aeon of fulfillment, but it does not mean the end of the fight of Christ. He continues His work and His fight against the evil forces in and through His Church. As far as the Church is the *regnum Christi* she has a share in the new aeon. But at the same time she lives her life in the old aeon. The Church is not the Kingdom of God, but in the present age she is called to be its medium and instrument. And therefore, just because it is the duty and the privilege of the Church to fight against all the hostile forces of evil working in mankind, she cannot take a negative position towards the life of Society without betraying the mission that has been entrusted to her.

I now turn to the question of the Christian conception of man. When it is said that this conception is not very suited for stimulating human activity, the basis of such a statement is the doctrine of the sinfulness of man and especially the idea of original sin. The consequence of this doctrine is thought to be that man cannot do anything "good" at all. When thus all the deeds of man are considered as sinful, this pessimistic view obviously cannot encourage man to work for a better condition of things in the world. It seems plausible here to find the explanation of the tendencies to leave "the world" and its problems out of consideration. Often it has been added that this pessimistic conception of human life has most strongly been unfolded by the Reformation and that therefore the Reformation is particularly responsible for the passivity of the Church.

The question now raised is a very complicated one. Certainly the Reformation holds a radical view as regards sin and evil. It is a central point in' the teaching of Luther as well as of Calvin that man has nothing to boast of before God and that, on the contrary, even his best deeds are sinful. Every possibility of self-justification is excluded. Justification is a gift of God, and not a result of the endeavors of man. Nevertheless, it would be a complete misinterpretation to say that, according to the reformers, men could not do anything "good." In fact, such an interpretation has been very common. But it is wrong. If we will understand what their teaching of man's sinfulness really means, we must clearly distinguish between two different points of view that are not to be confounded. As regards the relation of man to God it is strongly emphasized that man has no merits of his own. Before the face of God he is a sinner and nothing but a sinner. The judgment of God does not hit only this or that special deed, but it hits man wholly and entirely.

However, that does not mean that "natural man" could not do anything "good" in the ordinary sense of the word. The reformers distinguished between the justice that is valid before God, only existing as a gift of God, and the justice of the civil life, *iustitia civilis*. They have never intended to deny that man could be able to do things that ought here to be done, that were useful and, in a relative way, good and righteous according to the life of Society and its claims. As far as such actions served the will of God by establishing order out of chaos they were in harmony with "the Law" of the Creator. This view of the possibilities of "natural man" is obviously consistent with the view of St. Paul as expressed in the Epistle to the Romans: "For when the Gentiles, which have not the law, do by nature the things contained in the law, these, having not the law, are a law unto themselves." Therefore, the conception of the Reformation is not such a general blackening as is often maintained, especially since the time of the Enlightenment. But on the other side it is not an idealization of the progress of history. The possibilities of history are not only possibilities of good, but also of evil, and the possibilities of good are always relative—that is, according to the Reformation, applicable not only to "natural man" but also to Christian man. From this point of view, therefore, the incompleteness of all historic good appears an undeniable fact.

It is very deplorable that the important distinction between the justice before God and the *iustitia civilis*, the justice of history, has so often been overlooked especially through pietistic influences. That led to two fateful consequences: first to a limitation of the work of the Law, according to which the only purpose of the Law was to awake the consciousness of sin; secondly to a general blackening of the possibilities of man and thereby to a passive attitude towards Society. The Reformation on the other hand looked quite differently and far more positively upon these things. It never considered world and society as something profane, standing outside the world of God. The Reformation knew that this world, in spite of all, is the world of God where the Lord of the Creation and the Law is working, even through men who live outside the walls of an often isolated Church. The Law then was seen as a *dynamis* by which God Himself fights for "the good" against the evil forces of the world.

Indeed, the fact that the Church has been entrusted

with, and has responsibility for, the universal Law of God is the most fundamental reason why the Church never can be allowed to surrender to indifference towards Society. This fact quite simply condemns all theories that wish to isolate the Church. Of course the Church can stand apart, and undoubtedly she has not seldom stood apart, but she cannot take such a position without betraying her duty.

Before leaving the charges of passivity I feel myself obliged to say some words about the attitude of Luther. I must do that because in recent times he has often been made responsible for the weakness that Lutheran Churches have displayed in relation to the state. I will of course not deny that such a weakness has occurred, not least in Germany. Certainly, an indulgence of that kind is no specialty for Lutheran Churches, it can be found also in many other Churches to a great extent, for instance in orthodox Christendom. However, the serious thing is that Lutheran theologians in Germany, it could perhaps be said since the time of Bismarck, have defended the passivity of the Church in relation to the state and tried to base such theories upon Luther himself. The starting-point of these theologians has been Luther's famous distinction between the two governments, the "spiritual" and the "worldly," and his statement that these two governments have different purposes as well as different modes of action. From this basis theologians have concluded that the worldly government must act according to its own "laws," which may be quite different from the Law vindicated by the Church. A prominent German theologian some few years ago explained this theory by saying that the rule valid for the state must be to act according to "what is necessary for one's own people" (*die Lebensnotwendigkeit des eigenen Volkes*), and he even ventured to say that this view was characteristic for the "realistic" outlook of Luther. This theory, in fact a very pseudo-Lutheran one, considers only the following alternative: *either* a "Christian-theocratical" claim on state and policy, and then a confusion between the Realm of God and the worldly realms, *or* the so-called realistic outlook, just mentioned. The first possibility is being criticized because here a Christian disguise conceals a quite different un-Christian "political" policy. Moral verdicts substitute for political verdicts, and the critic emphasizes that nothing has more poisoned the relations between the peoples than such a moralization in the name of Christianity. A man who has learned from Luther cannot, it is said, take part in such proceedings. He has understood the "worldliness" of the policy, and therefore he avoids confusing political fronts with the front where God fights the devil. The result is that the second position must be chosen. The rule of the state must be "what is necessary for the life of the people."

The risks of this rule are obvious. Nothing prevents it from being transformed to pure self-assertion and unconcealed will to power. If in the first instance there was a risk that Christian phrases could conceal very suspicious actions, here there is no less risk for aspirations of power taking refuge behind the talk about what is necessary for the life of the people. However, this alternative does not exist for Luther himself. The so-called Christian-theocratical view could lead to a secularization of the Realm of God. The theory that the state ought to have its own "laws of necessity" leads to the secularization of the life of the state. They are both of them quite unfamiliar to Luther.

Speaking of the two different governments and their different purposes, Luther did not think that Church and State had nothing to do with each other. Even less he thought that the state ought to be free to act according to its own "laws" of necessity. It is his unshakably firm conviction that the state also has to obey the Law of God. When attributing to the state a divine purpose and considering it as a divine order, his reason was that the state, as the guardian of justice, is subordinated to the Law of God. Offending against this Law the state does not run God's but the devil's errands. According to Luther the temptation of the worldly government is that the power will be its own master and transform itself into God. It is, he says, "the work of the devil" that the ruling power shall occupy the supreme authority ("shall be *causa principalis*"), refusing to acknowledge the Creator and to remain His instrument.

Certainly we can find utterances of Luther where his loyalty towards "the worldly power" approaches servility, sometimes in connection with interpretations of Chapter 13 in the Epistle to the Romans. Nevertheless, his fundamental idea, as expressed in his doctrine of the two governments, is far from servile. He acknowledges no totalitarian government. When the worldly government misuses its power and offends against the Law of God, then it is the duty of the spiritual government to act. It has not to take over the tasks of the worldly government, but it has to "admonish the consciences," thus trying to awake the self-consciousness of the transgressors. That means, according to Luther, no interference from the side of the Church and no confusion of the two governments, but instead of that a realization of the purpose that belongs to the spiritual government: the Church fulfills her duty to watch over the sanctity of the Law of God. The Norwegian Churchmen in their hard fight had good reasons to refer to Luther—just as innumerable Lutherans had done before them throughout the ages.

Such is the position of Luther. It is, as we see, hugely different from the pseudo-Lutheran theory that praises Luther for his "realistic" view of political life. Certainly there are reasons for saying that his view was a realistic one. But his realism did not consist in a will to give up moral claims on the life of the state and so to promote its secularization, but instead of that in his clear and unconfused view of the sweeps of the demonic forces at work in our existence. Against these forces the State as well as the Church has to fight. The object of the fight is in both cases the demonism of power.

It has not at all been my intention to say that the problem of the relation between Church and State should have been in any way finally unraveled and solved by the thoughts of Luther here described. I have ventured only to demonstrate the inaccuracy of an interpretation maintaining that Luther's principal view and his doctrine of the two governments consequently should lead to an attitude of passivity and self-efface-ment of the Church.

Now we turn to the second type of charges against the Church, the accusations that the Church pretends a monopoly that cannot be justified and that therefore her activity leads to Utopian ideals.

When looking back at the activity of the Church in recent times as regards the life of Society, we could have reason to examine two different kinds of attitudes. One type is characterized by an attempt to amalgamate Christianity and general humanistic ideals. With such a syncretism as background it was usual to speak about "a social gospel." According to this view the Kingdom of God would be realized through improvements of the world's orders and systems. Social progress is con-sidered as a stage on the way towards perfection.

However, it is not neecssary here to criticize in detail this conception. It has been forced into the background, partly through our terrible experiences in the present time, partly through the self-consideration of theology and its deeper insight as to the essence of Christianity. It is obvious that the idea of a "social gospel" was nearly connected with an optimistic and perfectionist view of history that did not grasp the incompleteness of all historical good. So far the position is an Utopian one. It also is obvious that it is confusing in this way to speak about a social gospel. The Gospel is the Gospel of the grace of God, and this Gospel is quite different from social progress. Christianity would be changed into unrecognizability if these two things were confused. It would not elucidate but conceal the true relationships between Christianity and Society. In order not to be misunderstood I must add that the fault of this attitude, representative of modernism, is not its broad-mindedness nor its will in contact and co-operation with general humanism. On the contrary, such a co-operation is, as we shall see later, a necessity. But the fault is that it is sought in a way that Christianity cannot tread without losing its soul.

However, the exposition of the reasons for a Christian activity can follow a quite different line that, contrary to the conception just described, will emphasize Christianity as the only possible starting-point for bringing forth a better condition of things in the life of Society. It cannot be denied that in Christian quarters we not infrequently find a tendency to speak about these questions in a way that indicates a kind of monopoly for Christianity. At a cursory glance the argumentation seems to be rather convincing. The Christian Gospel, it is said, is the only rescue of the world. The only hope, the only solution of the needs and troubles of Society is men being regenerated, changed, earnestly Christianized. If only men would be truly Christianized, then it would not be beyond the means of humanity to manage its many burning problems. Only owing to that, something really good can be accomplished. Only so the divine Law can be fulfilled, and such a fulfillment is a necessary condition if the world shall be saved from decay, chaos and extinction.

In fact, such thoughts are very common. Then, is it not good and genuine Christianity? Or should there

really here exist reasons for talking about false pretensions and an illusionary outlook? Is it not rather just
what ought to be preached, especially in the present
situation? Are not such lines of thought suited to express Christianity's significance for Society?

Now it must of course not be denied that an argumentation of this kind contains an element of truth.
Few people would, I suppose, disavow that a true
Christian spirit is a spirit of righteousness, reconciliation and good will, and that, for a solution of difficult
problems, such a spirit must be available. Also it is
indisputable that a constant flood of justice, charity
and sacrificing service has emanated from this source.

All that being granted, nevertheless there are questions remaining. When examining the claims here raised
we find that the argumentation builds upon two assumptions. The first is that "natural man" cannot do
anything that is "good" and in accordance with the
divine Law; the second is that a Christian can fulfill
the divine Law and that he really fulfills it. The first
of these two statements we have already examined, and
then we found that it could not be justified. But also
the second statement cannot be vindicated from a
Christian point of view. It cannot be acquitted from
having performed an idealization of the Christian life,
its conditions and its possibilities. In fact, the more or
less perfectionist outlook corresponds neither to the
biblical view nor to reality. Certainly, the New Testament can speak with the most supreme expressions
about the change realized through the justification of
the sinner.

He is "holy," "righteous," "pure," he has got the gift
of the Holy Spirit, he has received the filiation of sons,
he is "a new creature: old things are passed away; be-
hold, all things are become new." (2 Cor. 5:17.) But
on the other side we find everywhere in the epistles as
well as in the gospels exhortations and admonitions
that often have reference to very elementary things.
Nothing is more obvious than the fact that the Christians, addressed by St. Paul, are far from faultless. The
explanation of this seeming contradiction is the truth
that the "holiness" and "sanctification" of the Christians,
according to the New Testament, is a religious reality,
given as a gift of God's grace, and not an ethical perfection. Human infirmity cannot destroy this religious
reality. But, on the other hand, the exhortations and
commandments tell man what he ought to do so as to
remain within this "holiness," and not through disobedience to the Holy Spirit to be excluded from grace.
Thus the sanctification and the responsibility of the
Christian are strongly emphasized. When later the Reformation in the famous formula that the Christian is
at the same time righteous and sinner accents the im-
perfection of the Christian life, that does not mean
anything new in relation to the view of the New Testament. It means only a keen, clear and accentuated expression of the conception already existing in the New
Testament. The formula in question stands up against
every tendency to idealize and gild the Christian life.
And the reality itself confirms beyond measure its truth.

In fact, nobody would for instance say that the Christians were superior to conflicts, party spirit, aspirations

of prestige *et cetera*. Nobody would say that the Christian Churches have always solved their own problems in an ideal way, without rivalry and on good terms. The history of the Church is full of mistakes and blunders. Then it seems to be far too pretentious, in spite of all such infirmities, to proclaim the solution of the entangled problems of the world as a Christian monopoly. Such an attitude cannot but challenge a criticism that very easily demonstrates the infirmities of the Christian life, the individual life as well as the life of the Church.

Looking back at the theory now discussed we must acknowledge the merit that is to be found in its efforts to call the Christian life to social activity. Thereby it has accomplished an achievement that ought not to be underestimated. On the other side, its fault lies in the tendency to monopolize this activity for converted and confessing Christians. The background of this attitude is the thought that only the regenerated man can perform the will of God, and that he also really performs it. The first statement is not true, and the second is only half a truth.

Obviously this line of thought, that may be indicated as a pietistic one, is characterized by an exclusiveness that must isolate Christianity from those considered as standing outside, from the world considered as profane. So far as these tendencies are effective, they cannot but further the process of secularization. The relation between Christianity and Society here is thought of neither as a relation to Society as such, nor as an immediate relation. It is thought of only as a relation that passes through Christian individuals and their work as intermediary links. While the modernist view had open eyes for the danger of exclusiveness, but found no other way to overcome it except through a reinterpretation of Christianity that in fact meant a process of disintegration, the pietistic view, on the other side, frightened by this attitude, found no way of establishing contact with the humanity outside Christianity and therefore stopped in a position of antithesis. The deepest reason for this exclusiveness lies in the fact that the Law of God was not given the place belonging to it by right. The question about the relation between Christianity and Society is foremost a question about the Law of God and its universal claim. Therefore, a self-examination of the Church must lead to an investigation as regards the due place of the Law in Christianity.

IV

THE PLACE OF THE LAW IN CHRISTIAN TEACHING

IN the previous chapters I have at certain points suggested that the relations between Church and Society have suffered from the fact that the Law has been forced aside and thus has not been allowed to function according to its design. The situation was not improved if, on the other hand, Christianity was interpreted in a moralizing way. That meant only that neither Gospel nor Law was able to act according to its designs. Considering these circumstances, we very well understand Luther's famous statement that one of the most important trials of theology concerns its ability "rightly to deal Law and Gospel." In fact, this question has been one of the most burning questions of theology ever since the appearance of Christianity.

When asking why a theology that is eager to vindicate the pure gospel of salvation has often been led to reduce the importance of the Law, and even to antinomistic attitudes, the answer is not difficult to find. We must not forget that Christianity from its very beginning appeared as a contrast to the Jewish religion of Law. The words and actions of Jesus, according to the gospels, everywhere testify this opposition. The central teaching of St. Paul about the justification of man is a clear and intense antithesis to all kinds of legalistic religion. And St. John says: "The Law was given by Moses, but grace and truth came by Jesus Christ." Considering this antithesis, it is not surprising that in the history of Christianity we find temptations to abolish "the Law" and to maintain that its time has passed. But obviously that could not be the solution of the problem. Jesus said that he had come not to destroy the Law but to fulfill it; St. Paul asserts that the Law is "holy," and St. John eagerly teaches the commandment of Love. It is said to be a "new commandment" and at the same time "no new commandment, but an old commandment which ye had from the beginning" (1 John 2:7–8).

Therefore, it is evident that the attitude of the New Testament towards the Law is a double-sided one. From one point of view the Law has been dethroned. It has lost its claim. There exists a dominion where the Law has no rights and where the gospel of salvation rules with unlimited power. But from another point of view the Law remains in all its authority and sovereignty. However, this regulation of the boundaries does not mean that Gospel and Law should now be considered as two quantities that have nothing to do with each other. On the contrary, they are closely united. In fact, we could here apply the famous Chalcedonian formula about the relations between the two natures of Christ: "without confusion, without change, without division, without separation." The risk on the one hand is that the sovereignty of the Law or the Gospel may be limited and then that the two great powers are confused or changed; on the other hand that they may be separated from each other, for instance so that the Christian life is thought existing without Law, in other words: antinomistic theories obscure the claims of the Law. Here we are meeting some very important questions. The first is: in what sense has the Law been dethroned through the Gospel?

*　　　*　　　*

St. Paul speaks of the Law as an "enemy" and of the salvation and the justification of man as a release from the power of the Law, from the thralldom under the Law. In like manner Luther describes the Law as a "tyrant." For Luther as well as for St. Paul, the hostile forces of evil were not only sin, death and devil; the Law also belonged to them. From the tyranny of these enemies Christ saved us through His victory. Now it is not surprising that expressions like these can easily lead to false conclusions. Therefore it is necessary to see what exactly the thought of the Law as a defeated enemy means and what it does not mean. Obviously it means a radical and most accentuated opposition to all legalistic religion. If the Law is considered as a way to salvation, then the Law, that as such is holy and good, will be an enemy and a destructive force. Then it leads not to God, but away from God. As a way of salvation the Law has been defeated and abolished through the victory of Christ. It has no more any voice in the matter of salvation. Instead of that, salvation is altogether a gift of God, having its foundation only in the gospel of grace that is God's *dynamis* to salvation. The accusations of the Law become silent when man is justified alone by the grace of God. Here the Law has no condemning power. It cannot call in question or jeopardize the fullness of God's forgiveness. The Law is abolished *in loco justificationis,* but also *only in loco justificationis.* Otherwise the Law stands holy and firm in its majesty as expression of the unchangeable will of God Himself.

The intention of St. Paul as well as of the Reformation was to preach a "pure Gospel." And it ought never to be denied in the Church that the pure Gospel is the heart of Christianity. Moreover, the Gospel as opposed to a legalistic religion is not a specialty of St. Paul, it is the message of the whole of the New Testament. Because the Reformation had many experiences of a moralization of Christianity behind itself, it was very eager to keep watch to hinder the Law, that had been excluded from the sanctuary of justification, from re-entering through a back door. Even as justification could not be attained by any deeds of man, just so little could performances of justified men be merits for the final salvation. Such an idea would have meant among other things a sinfulness of human deeds that the Reformation could not accept. Therefore, the famous formula that man justified is at the same time righteous and sinner (*simul justus et peccator*) served as a guardian against all attempts of the Law to re-enter through a back door. Certainly, the Reformation would strongly vindicate that justification through the grace of God gives man new power to work according to the will of God as expressed in His Law. But it would at the same time deny that salvation was dependent on such human deeds, dependent on a *fides caritate formata,* as it was said in the Middle Ages. On the contrary, salvation is primary in relation to all performances of the Law. It has its own sovereignty and needs no complement. Every thought of a complement would be a confusion of Gospel and Law, of salvation and human performances.

The message of the New Testament and also of the Reformation is not that man would be unable in any way to perform the Law, but, instead of that, that the way of the Law is no way to salvation and, therefore, that even a complete performance of the Law would not lead to salvation. Certainly, the performance of the Law is always, also for Christians, a relative one. But the inefficiency of the Law as a way to salvation is not dependent upon the shortcomings as regards the performance of the Law. The Law is on the whole no way of salvation, and it is not intended to be such a way. It has quite another function to accomplish.

*   *   *

Then our second question must be: *What exactly is the function of the Law?* Which is the dominion where the Law, excluded from justification, acts with unshortened and full majesty? The most common answer as regards the function of the Law certainly is that the Law convinces of sin, that it awakens the consciousness of sin and leads man to repentance. No Christian will deny the fact that the Law acts in this manner or that this conception corresponds to the biblical view. Here sin is unveiled, not only as moral defects and transgressions, but as something that concerns "the heart," the deepest and most concealed intentions of the human mind. Sin appears as an egotism from which we cannot deliver ourselves, and therefore as the mighty force that enslaves humanity and here exercises its dominion. Sin means, according to the famous expression of Luther, that man is *incurvatus in se*, selfishly bended into himself, seeking his own, and that there is no sin so treacherous as when man seeks his own even in religion, making himself the center of existence and considering God and his gifts as a means of obtaining the supreme good. As regards the life of society, man can very well perform deeds that are useful, good and righteous in the ordinary sense of the words, but before the eye of God all righteousness and all merits disappear as snow before the sun. Before God, man is a sinner and nothing but a sinner.

But if, therefore, we undubitably meet here a central function of the Law, it is quite another question if that is the Law's only function. In a pamphlet belonging to the ecumenical correspondence where the relation of the Church to the international reconstruction was discussed, I found the following statement: "The teaching of the Law can, according to the biblical view, only be a help for the world so far as it leads to recognition of sin." This pronouncement is very typical. It is, in fact, characteristic for a whole epoch. Exactly in this manner it was argued when the Church was isolated from the life of the world and that life was surrendered to a quite profane interpretation. Then it was always said that the only function of the Law was to convince of sin. But the Church, in old times as well as at the time of the Reformation and later, had good reasons to speak in a different way.

Our fathers, from the time of the Reformation and their successors, used to speak about two functions of the Law, about a *primus usus* and a *secundus usus*. The "second" function concerned its power to convince of sin. The "first" function, on the other side, meant the foundation that God through His Law has established for the living together of humanity. And it is not true that this conception of the Law lacks biblical basis. The Bible, the New Testament as well as the Old, knows very well what the Law means as a foundation of human fellowship, what it means for suppressing evil and bending the insubordinate and creating order out of chaos.

When speaking about this "first function" of the Law, the theologians naturally had foremost in view the commandments of the Bible. But at the same time they knew that God had not left Himself without witness even for peoples that had not got the Law of the commandments. As the Law of the Creator it was a universal Law that appeared in God's deeds, but then has been testified and elucidated in God's holy Word. From this point of view God has two instruments for fighting the evil of the world: the Gospel and the Law. Just as the Gospel is a *dynamis* unto salvation, so is the Law a *dynamis* unto the establishment of human fel-

lowship. The Law is a force that contests and subdues
the destructive forces in humanity and that lays the
foundation necessary for maintaining human fellowship, in the first place then, the foundation of justice.
Thus, justice is not only something relative, changing
according to the changing human situations and claims.
The claim of justice is superior to all human order and
organizations, holy and inviolable.

*   *   *

It is impossible to speak about these things without
at least touching upon the much-debated question of
the *so-called natural Law, lex naturae*. This phrase, as
is well known, has a long history, going back to ancient
times. It was accepted by the mediaeval Church, it
was, in a different way, used by the reformers and it
is continually used by the Roman Catholic Church.
In the seventeenth and eighteenth centuries *lex naturae*
appeared in a secularized shape and acted for some
time as a kind of substitute, when theology more and
more lost sight of "the first function" of the divine Law.
Lex naturae was then thought to contain definite moral
norms, resting on a rational basis and including certain
human rights of universal applicability. As long as "the
natural Law" was in power, it worked as a universal
principle of right and was considered as a rational and
self-evident foundation of social order. However, by
and by, this conception of *lex naturae* was subjected
to a criticism that led to its dissolution. From a general
philosophical point of view it may be possible to vindicate the category of right as an inescapable category.

But it is not possible rationally to demonstrate a definite content of the consciousness of right. When then the ideological background for human communion on the foundation of the consciousness of right ceased to exist, that meant at the same time that the consciousness of right was subjected to a continuing process of disintegration. Instead of a general idea of a definite right, there was only place for different ideas trying to vindicate themselves by fighting against each other.

It is not surprising that in the present time, which has witnessed such a terrible decline of the sense of righteousness, voices are heard that plead the cause of "the natural Law," or that at least require a substitute for this Law. However, the natural Law cannot be revived either as a rational principle of right or as definite human rights, valid for all times and in all situations. Therefore Protestant theology cannot return to the Roman Catholic way of advocating the natural Law. Nevertheless, it has every reason to consider not only what in old time was called the first function of the Law, but also the universal perspective that appeared when the Law was thought of as the Law of the Creator.

This perspective has been compromised in two ways. First because it has been combined with the idea of a so-called natural theology, and secondly because recently it has been misused by some theories as regards so-called orders of creation, which have been identified with actual, historical orders, thus being falsely considered as sacrosanct. Against the theory of a natural theology, it has rightly been said, that the Bible knows only one way to God, the way through Jesus Christ. But here it also must be vindicated that the alternative, *either* revelation only through Christ *or* a natural revelation and a natural knowledge of God, is a false alternative, not corresponding to the biblical view of revelation. Although Christ, according to the Bible, is the only way to God, the Bible does not think that God has revealed Himself only in Christ. God also has revealed Himself through the Law. Even the Gentiles are, as St. Paul says, "the Law unto themselves" and "the wrath of God is revealed from heaven against all ungodliness and unrighteousness of men, who hold the truth in unrighteousness" (Rom. 1:18). The alternative, here mentioned, is false because, according to the Bible, the revelation is not thought of as a theoretical source of knowledge, but rather as a *dynamis* revealing God's mighty deeds. From this point of view the Law is seen just as a *dynamis,* working in the human world. The Law is not a way to God beside Christ, it is on the whole no way to God. But it is an instrument through which God realizes His will in human life, fighting against the evil forces ravaging there.

* * *

The difference between the "natural Law" and the Christian view of God's Law is now obvious. The natural Law is an idea of certain moral norms and statements, the idea of a general, rational human conscience. On the contrary, the biblical view of God's Law means that the living God, through His actions, reveals His will and His righteousness. It means at the same time that man, acting against the will of God, also acts against His destiny and mission, in a direction towards His own destruction and towards chaos and desolation in the world. The will of God, thus revealed in His Law, is nothing but the will of His Love. The Law no less than the Gospel is an expression of His Love. God's will is that men shall live "in love" to each other, and not in selfishness. Thus St. Paul can say that all the "commandments" are "comprehended in that saying: thou shalt love thy neighbor as thyself." From this point of view the Law of God is not primarily a series of statements, but a way of living. It is the *dynamis* that aims at and leads men to take care of their neighbors. The care in question concerns all human relations and is in an equal degree directed towards individuals and to the community. This universal claim is then the fundamental principle of the justice that God erects as regards the human fellowship. It must be strongly emphasized that here love and justice cannot be separated from each other, and still less, as often has happened, be considered as an antithesis. To this subject I will return. Now I will only establish that the justice, embodied in the Law of God, is nothing but the actual and realistic care of one's neighbor that is the central meaning of the love in question.

It is important, not least from the point of view of the relation between Church and Society, to lay stress upon the universality of the Law as here described. If the idea of the natural Law cannot be maintained and no rational foundation of a binding right can be vindicated, then it is more necessary than ever that Christianity sincerely considers its unshirkable responsibility before the Law of the Creator, and also that it does not forget its universal perspective, protecting from a false exclusiveness and narrow-sightedness which has often obscured and harmed the Church's attitude to Society.

Before leaving the question about the place of the Law in Christian teaching, it is necessary to investigate more closely the *Law's relation to the Christian life*. I need hardly say that in this matter you can find the most diversified views. You can find the idea that there is a higher Law, a *nova lex*, for Christians, but also the idea that the Law, having been abolished through justification, is no more applicable to Christians, their life being characterized by spontaneous works of love. You can find antinomistic or perfectionist or even narrow casuistic views. On one side it can be said that Christians have a special Law, on the other side that they don't need any Law at all, and that they, as justified, are liberated from the Law.

Considering this complex of questions, we must first state that the Law of God is one and indivisible, just as the will of God always remains the same. There are not two different kinds of Law, one higher and one lower. There exists only one universal Law, applicable to all mankind. Christ is a Saviour and not a new lawmaker. He is the fulfiller of the Law, not only through His work, but also as interpreting the Law and revealing its deepest sense. But the Law that He interprets in word and deed is no other than the universal Law of the Creator, that "was from the beginning." He helps us to a deeper insight into this Law, but He does not fix the Law in paragraphs and statements valid for all situations. The pronouncements in the Sermon on the Mount ought not to be understood as such legal statements, valid for all occasions in the life of Society, but as explanations of the sense of the Creator's Law of Love. The interpretation of the Sermon on the Mount as legislation of universal applicability has only obscured the sense of the Law, especially when the Sermon on the Mount was considered as the "social gospel" of Christianity. That meant a complete confusion of Law and Gospel.

Because there exists only one Law, and not a higher Law for Christians and a lower one for other people, there is no place for a double morality. Thoughts in this direction have appeared, as is well known, in different forms in Christendom. But they are all excluded through the fact that the Law is one and indivisible. Quite another thing is that there is, of course, room for different stages as regards the fulfillment of the Law. The Law can be fulfilled more or less with a willing heart, and more or less under constraint. However, the Christian knows only too well that the fulfillment of the Law always is a relative one. He knows better than anybody that all his thoughts, words and deeds are burdened with sin, and that there does not exist anything in his life that must not be submitted to the judgment of God.

Then, what indeed does the Law mean for the Christian? In what sense is he liberated from the Law? For a radical and realistic view of Christianity it is necessary to beware of all idealizations and gildings as well as frankly to express the richness that in fact belongs to the Christian life. The Christian life is exposed to two opposite temptations, the temptation to presumption and the temptation to desperation.

When the Bible speaks about the Christian's liberation from the Law, that means, as we have already seen, that the Law has no voice in the matter of justification, *in loco justificationis*. Here the power of the Law has been completely abolished, but also only here. The forgiveness of God is a complete forgiveness. The Law has no right to condemn him whom God has justified. "Who shall lay anything to the charge of God's elect? It is God that justifieth. Who is he that condemneth" (Rom. 8:33–34). As far as man is justified through the incomprehensible mercy of God, he is liberated from the power of the Law. But that does not mean that the Law should have nothing to do with the Christian life. On the contrary, the freedom that belongs to the Christian life is a freedom from the legalistic religion, from the legalistic relation to God. The spiritual freedom, "the freedom of the Spirit," is a freedom from the Law as far as the Law is an "enemy," a hostile and destructive force, a "law of sin" in the words of St. Paul. But it is not a freedom from the holy and sovereign Law of God.

In fact, in the Christian life also the Law acts in both of its functions, as convincing of sin and as a *dynamis*, challenging and driving to works of love. The judging work of the Law, its power to convince of sin and to lead to penance is not only a preparatory work, preceding the remission of sins. It is not a work that is done once for all as an introduction to the Christian life. On the contrary, it belongs to the Christian life as long as we live on earth. The deeper man enters into the Christian life, the more this function of the Law is strengthened, the more man is sanctified, the more his eyes are opened for even the most concealed and hidden ways of sin. He sees more clearly than ever that he is not only "a new man," justified through the grace of God, but also "an old man," that his fight against sin will never cease during his earthly life, that he has no merits of his own to present before God and that every day he needs God's forgiveness. At the same time the Law acts as a *dynamis* towards activity in the service of God. Here the Law is now inseparably united with the Gospel. If as regards justification, Gospel and Law must not be confused, if then they must be clearly distinguished from each other, here the situation is quite different. Now the watchword is: "without separation." When, for instance, St. Paul says: "the love of Christ constraineth us" (2 Cor. 5:14), that indicates the union of Gospel and Law, here to be found. That means not only an intensified view of the Law as the Law of love, but also that the Law is now seen from a new outlook, as "the Law of freedom."

But it is then important to see what "freedom" here really means. Obviously it can neither mean that man is free to take the course of his own will and desires, nor an individualistic freedom of isolation and self-sufficiency. The Christian freedom loses its sense if it is not considered as, by implication, being bound to God and

His will. Therefore the New Testament, when speaking about freedom, at the same time speaks about obedience. Freedom thus means liberation to service. From this point of view the "freedom of the Spirit" is obedience to the Spirit, to the commands that it actualizes and leads us to find out. The Law of love, its conclusive and comprehensive claim, is then brought to life and made concrete and definite in the different occasions and situations man is confronted with. I could here quote some expressive words from a new Swedish hymn:

> The life of the Spirit He lights in us.
> When we obey, he leads us on,
> Sends us into deeds
> That He prepares day by day.

We cannot acquire salvation through obedience, but on the other hand we cannot live the life of salvation without obedience, we lose it through disobedience.

When the New Testament speaks of the *agape* working through Christians, or when the Reformation, and especially Luther, speaks of the spontaneity that characterizes Christian love in action, the intention is to indicate that men are acting as instruments of the divine *agape* itself. Therefore, such statements would be misunderstood and lead to a false idealization of the Christian life and its conditions, if the spontaneity in question should be considered primarily as a human quality. From a psychological point of view, the Christian life and activity obviously cannot be characterized simply as a free, unchecked sparkling and spontaneous love, acting without resistance. Such a gilding of the reality would be to eliminate obedience and to separate the Law from the Gospel of grace. The "spontaneity" is not any newly acquired human quality. It is no human quality at all. The spontaneity belongs wholly and entirely to the divine *agape*** itself and to the spirit that overmasters man and his resistance, leading him to a service of willingness.

Thus, the Law of the Creator and the justification alone by the grace of God are united in a firm alliance. Because the Gospel rules alone *in loco justificationis*, because every legalistic view as regards the way to God has been abolished, the Law has been liberated to work according to its own purpose. When the Law is no more used in a false way for bringing forth human merits and justice before God, then it appears in all its majesty and power. The false use of the Law had robbed it of its power and changed it from a friend to an enemy. Now the activity of the Law is led in the right direction; it is directed to the service of human fellowship. Now it is obvious that man cannot serve God in any other way than by serving his fellow-creatures. All activity, promoted by the *dynamis* of the Law is working for this purpose: for realizing the Creator's Law of *agape* in human fellowship, as well negatively as positively, not only by fighting the evil and destructive forces in human life, but also, and foremost, by constructive work for a true communion. That says the decisive word about the duty and responsibility of the

*Agape "is primarily divine, not human, love." N. F. S. Ferré, *Evil and the Christian Faith*, p. 148.

Church in relation to Society. Only it must be added that the work of the *agape* here requested cannot be separated from the claims of justice. The actions of the *agape* are not a supererogatory work, not a complement to justice, they correspond exactly to the claims of justice.

Still another question! We have laid stress upon the universality of the Law and upon the relativity of its fulfillment. That means two things, first that God does not work through His Law only in the Christian sphere; secondly that the relativity as regards the fulfillment belongs also to the Christian life. What is then indeed the importance of Christianity for the position of the Law and for the Christian attitude towards its claim? How is the influence of Christianity to be described?

Concerning the question of the position of the Law, our answer must be first that Christianity, as we already have seen, gives a deeper, a fuller insight into the sense of the Law of love; secondly, that the claim of justice is now definitely elevated over all relativizing tendencies. While we cannot vindicate that the sovereignty of justice would only be in force within the Christian sphere, nevertheless we must assert that for Christians all relativizing tendencies must be excluded, because here the Law is an expression of God's unchangeable will.

As regards the question of the Christian attitude, our answer is that the characteristic features of the Christian mind are humility and confidence. Because the Christian must know that, even at best, his fulfillment of the Law is a very relative one, that he has nothing at all to boast of and that all his life with all his works is submitted to the judgment of God, superciliousness and self-content ought never to be found in the Christian mind. They have no right to make their voices heard. On the other hand, the Christian attitude ought to be an attitude of confidence. Confidence and faith belong together. The confidence of the Christian mind is legitimate because the Christian does not live only under God's judgment, but also under His grace, because he receives the gift of the divine forgiveness and has got membership in "the Kingdom that cannot be moved."

Therefore, the Christian outlook on history must be a double-sided one. It cannot be an outlook either of presumption or of despair. The attitude of Utopian idealization is excluded because the Christian knows far too well the power of the evil and destructive forces and the relativity of all good works performed by men. But on the other hand, history is not a meaningless process. It is a drama where victories can be won against the evil forces. It is led towards a goal that cannot be frustrated. The time of the present age is a time of possibilities, and these possibilities are, according to the Christian faith, God's own possibilities. When Jesus says: "As my Father has continued working to this hour, so I work too," then "to this hour" does not mean only for a time, but for all ages and generations.

V

THE LAW OF GOD AND JUSTICE

WE have indicated that, from the Christian point of view, the Law of God as the Law of the Creator is the source and foundation of justice. But is that really true? The Law of God is the Law of love. But is not justice something quite different from love? That seems for instance to be the argumentation of Emil Brunner in his book on *Justice and the Social Order*. Justice is here described as the principle of *suum cuique*. Love on the other hand lives on a higher level. Justice is to give every man his due. It has altogether a rational basis. But love is not rational. It loves even the unworthy, and it does not do only what it is bidden to do, but far more. In the life of Society, there does not exist anything higher than Justice. Love does not know anything about the order of Society. So far Brunner agrees with Karl Barth: "the State does not know anything about love." According to this view, therefore, the Law of love and justice are sharply distinguished from each other. It would be impossible to speak about the Law of God as the foundation of justice.

When examining this fundamental question, let us first remember what has previously been said about the Law. We have conceived the Law as *dynamis*, as a divine power working in human history, creating order out of chaos, and judging unrighteousness. This divine Law, therefore, is not a series of statements and fixed rules, valid for every situation. Nevertheless, its character is quite clear. The compass is reliable, its deflexions infallible. It is no accidental occurrence that the Bible over and over again says that the entire Law is summed up in the words: "Thou shalt love thy neighbor as thyself."

Now, can it really be maintained that this claim would have relation to justice as it ought to be realized in the life of Society? I do not hesitate to give an affirmative answer.

When examining "the Law of love" in the beginning we must observe that "love" appears in many different shapes and degrees, according to the different personal relations. Therefore, it would not be advisable to define the Law of love only according to the most intimate personal relations. Nor would it be appropriate to describe the manifestations of love only or chiefly as strong and intense affections. In fact, the famous formula "to love our neighbors as ourselves" must be considered as a guardian against all more or less sentimental views of love. The words "as thyself" obviously cannot mean that we ought to cherish ourselves with strong and intense affections. Such an interpretation forbids itself. The formula in question can only mean in a real and actual way to take care of the gift of the life that has been given to us, to take charge of and realize its possibilities. In the same realistic, sober and substantial way we ought to take care of our neighbors. That being the case, the Law of love obviously has direct relations to all the life of Society. The primary and fundamental manifestation of the Law of love is just this positive and matter-of-fact care for human fellowship in all its relations, and that is at the same time the fundamental claim of justice and righteousness. We can leave it an open question if on the whole there exist any supererogatory works of love, if indeed love can do anything but its duty. However, what is requested by the Law of love is primarily and fundamentally nothing but the care here described. And exactly this care is at the same time the fundamental principle of justice.

In fact, one runs a great risk to separate justice and love and to accent the difference between them. The risk is that love will be sentimentalized, and that justice will shrink to a shadow of its true self. It is no accidental occurrence that Brunner has taken his formula of justice from Aristotle and that he speaks of a rational basis of justice. That means that his eyes are directed towards *lex naturae*. But such a basis is not only very uncertain, but also far too small for supporting the whole structure of justice.

Justice may very well be considered as the highest thing in the life of Society. Indeed, nothing can be more fundamental for a State than to maintain an order of justice. But then it is important that justice is not isolated from the life-giving *dynamis* of the Law whose main principle is the care of "one's neighbors" and of the fellowship as a whole. Such a statement is not an abstract speculation without reference to reality. When looking at the endeavors in the present life of Society, we certainly find many great dangers and risks. But at the same time it is obvious that we also, more than ever before, find eager attempts to overcome injustices and anomalous states of things in the social life: attempts to take care of all the members of Society and, as far as possible, to make their position and circumstances safe. However, these endeavors are not to be characterized as a work of charity, and far less as incidental measures of assistance. On the contrary, the leading principle without any doubt is the principle of justice. The intention is, as far as possible, to realize the claims of justice and righteousness in Society. If you like, you may describe this principle as the principle of *suum cuique*, but only if, at the same time, you interpret it in accordance with the Law whose central function is to bring forth a realistic care of "one's neighbor," of the life of Society as a whole. The tendency is more and more to build Society as a Society of justice and right. But the justice, thus fought for, is a manifestation of the Law of love. So far, the State obviously knows something about love.

It is, however, possible that you will now make an objection against this argumentation. Probably you will not deny that there exist actions of justice that at the same time are actions of love. But you will, perhaps, assert that justice at times must act against the Law of love, as for instance when justice acts as a punishing justice. At a cursory glance, such reasoning may seem uncontradictable. But a closer investigation will, I think, change the outlook. First we must take into consideration that love very well can, and sometimes also must, use very severe means. To overlook this fact would be to sentimentalize love. In any case the Christian view of love is something quite different from weakness and indulgence. Certainly it cannot be denied that punishments executed in the name of justice have very often in the history of mankind been quite contrary to the Law of love, that they for instance have been nothing but manifestations of an unchecked revenge. But, indeed, that kind of activity cannot rightly be described as justice. It is only a caricature.

It is a claim of the Law of love that human fellowship shall not be surrendered without protection to human brutality as well as it is also a claim of the same Law that the punishment shall not have the character of vengeance, resting on self-satisfaction, and that it shall also, as far as possible, try to lead the offender to better ways. Thus, the punishment of justice has clearly to draw the dividing line between good and evil actions. It is a claim of the Law of love that evil action shall be branded. But it is also a claim of the same Law that the punishment, as far as possible, shall try to win the offender back to the life of Society. Therefore, if justice shall maintain its character of real justice, it is in fact obvious that the source and foundation of justice cannot be found anywhere but in the Law of love.

The source and foundation of justice have now been

determined as the Creator's Law that is universal and
unconditional, the manifestation of which is, in a
positive and realistic way, to take care of "our neighbors," of the human fellowship as a whole. From this
point of view it is most important to emphasize then
that the principle of justice appears as a *claim*, acting
as a compass as regards the realization of justice in the
life of Society. The importance of this view may perhaps best come to light, if it is compared with two
other methods of vindicating the foundation of justice,
the references either to "human rights" or to "human
dignity."

When the foundation of justice is bound up with the
idea of human rights, it is usualy thought that there
exist some human rights belonging to human nature.
These rights being considered as definite and unconditional, the background is obviously the idea of the
natural Law, that sometimes, as for instance in the
famous Declaration of Independence of the United
States of America, can also be apprehended as "the
Law of Nature's God." Here it is said: "We hold these
truths to be self-evident, that all men are created equal,
that they are endowed by their Creator with certain
inalienable rights; that among these are life, liberty
and the pursuit of happiness." This idea of the human
rights is here the starting-point of justice, the reason
for its sovereignty and the foundation of the life of
Society as a whole.

Now it is not at all my intention to say anything
depreciatory about the endeavors to fix and defend
such human rights. When similar endeavors have been

attempted even in our own time, in the time of the world-crisis, we could not but consider them as a gleam of light in the dark hours. Indeed, the attempts to fix and defend "human rights" undoubtedly have been and still may be a help in the fight for the cause of justice. But at the same time it would scarcely be advisable to consider certain fixed human rights as an unshakable foundation of justice and as a safe protection against all relativization. The content of human rights will always be interpreted in different ways. And not only that. The conceptions of human rights have changed in the course of the ages, and they will always change according to different situations and times. Therefore, if the Law of justice is quite simply to be identified with certain, once-for-all-given human rights, that would mean that the principle of justice should be submitted to a continuing process of relativization. The Law as a claim, on the other side, has possibilities of a different type. The claim is primary and superior in relation to all human rights. Only such a claim can be elevated over all relativizing tendencies, and owing to that serve as the fundamental principle of justice.

However, it seems that in recent times, the idea of *human dignity* has played an even more important role than the idea of human rights. The human dignity, the value that belongs to every man, has been considered as the foremost safeguard against the mechanization as well as the brutalization of life, and thus as the true basis of justice. Men ought never to be treated in a way that violates their high value and honor. The primary function of justice ought to be to ward off all treatment of men contrary to human dignity.

This idea has different sources. To a large extent it has grown up in humanism and philosophical idealism, in the Renaissance and in the idealism of the nineteenth century. But of course it also has references to Christianity. Some biblical statements are very often quoted in this connection, for instance the pronouncement of man as created in the image of God and the words of Jesus that man is worth more than the birds or his question: "What does it profit a man, to gain the whole world and forfeit his life?" Also, it has often been said that the most distinctive feature as regards the Christian view of man is the idea of the infinite worth of the soul of man.

Undoubtedly, this idea of the dignity of man has rendered excellent services in reference to the care claimed by the Law of love. It has awakened and inspired the conscience. But quite another question is if it can be considered as the fundamental principle of justice. Concerning its relations to Christianity, the Bible certainly emphasizes "the value" of the human soul, at first hand seen from the point of view of God's design and man's responsibility. However, at the same time we must observe that the Law of love, claiming us to take care of our "neighbors" is never motivated by reference to any human dignity, to the worth and value of the neighbor for whom we ought to care. On the contrary, every reflection in such a direction is completely excluded. The claim positively to take care of the human fellowship is unconditional. It is simple duty. Nothing can be more unfamiliar to the biblical view than the opinion that our attitude and actions in relation to our fellow-men should be motivated and justified by their inherent worth and value and by human dignity on the whole.

There is no reason to depreciate the idea of human dignity and worth. Nevertheless, whatever importance this view may have, it would be very risky to consider it as the foundation of justice. If it does not have the religious basis that we find in the New Testament, but instead of that is defended with rational arguments, then the relativizing tendencies are not only near at hand, but in fact inevitable. When mankind is seen from a rational point of view nothing can be more obvious than the fact that men have very different values. Looking at this sliding scale of values from the outlook of Society, it must be stated that some men have a higher value than others in the life of Society, and also that there exist men who have a minimal value, or even no value at all. This relativizing view opens the way towards an attitude that completely neglects and despises men considered as inferior. We are confronted with the "master-moral," the terrible results of which we have experienced beyond measure in our time. Therefore, because the rational idea of human dignity, dealing with varying values, is permanently tempted to dangerous relativizations, it cannot be maintained as the principle of a sovereign justice. In order to be able to serve the cause of justice, the idea of human dignity and worth must be subordinated to the universal claim of the Law, that is unconditional

and therefore independent of viewpoints of value and
dignity. Thus, it may be all right to advocate "human
rights" and "human dignity," but the claim of the Law
must be superior to both of them.

Returning then to the claim of the Law, interpreted
in a positive and realistic way to care for "our neighbors," we must now take into consideration some characteristic features of this principle, regarded in relation
to justice. Here we must start from our description of
the Law as a *dynamis,* as a claim and as a compass.
The principle in this case is a critical principle. It is,
of course, not possible simply to deduce definite, fixed
statements and paragraphs of Law valid for all ages
for our principle. The Law-making of Society is subjected to a permanent development and transformation.
New situations demand new legislations. Such legislations must be drawn up according to the actual situations in Society and their possibilities. But that does
not mean that the principle here would have no function. On the contrary, it must act just as a critical principle, critical not only in a negative way, but also and
foremost in a positive and constructive way.

From this point of view our claim is characterized
by activity and mobility, elasticity. The claim in a
realistic way to care for "our neighbors" means that
the activity of the Church cannot be reduced only to
a defensive position, to an opposition against actions
of violence and brutality from the side of the State.
It means also that the activity of the Church cannot
be confined only to charity. Certainly, the Church will
always have plenty of place for actions of charity and

for Samaritan works. And functions of this kind obviously belong to the inescapable duty of the Church. But the Church will not act according to the Law of God, if she confines her activity to being only a guardian against aggression or a helper in situations of misery. If the central function of the Law is in a realistic way to care for the human fellowship, then it has a direct reference to the life of Society, to the construction and constitution of Society. The "love" here requested by the Law must in the first place be justice and righteousness. It must act as a living conscience, fighting for the intentions of the Law in perpetually new situations. The direction of this activity is constant. Its purpose is unchangeable. But at the same time the principle in function can never be steadfastly tied to social and political theories of one kind or another, for instance neither to Conservative nor to Communist views. On the contrary, the greatest possible mobility and elasticity are needed. The eyes of the Church must be turned to all changing possibilities that allow an application of the principle.

When the principle then is confronted with the varying political and social theories, its constructive criticism concerns not least the relation between the individual and the community. The claim of "taking care of one's neighbors" is directed just as much to the entirety as to the particular man. It turns as well against an isolating and self-sufficient individualism as against an enslaving collectivism. I need scarcely say that the problem here touched upon is fundamental for the life of Society, nor that in the history of mankind the antithesis between individualism and collectivism has played and, not least in our own time, plays a decisive role. Looking at this history, we get primarily the impression of a permanent fight between the two rivals. Obviously in this fight the most precious values are at stake. The watchword of individualism is liberty. And certainly liberty has a very precious value. But an individualism, endeavoring with every conceivable means to vindicate self-interest, is destructive to the life of Society, whether it is an individualism of the particular individual or a class individualism. Not every freedom is a glorious freedom, in any case not the liberty that lets greediness for power dominate over willingness to serve, and thus reveals in its actions the demon of power.

But the same demon of power appears no less when an enslaving and terrorizing collectivism takes the place of destructive individualism. Then you may talk glorious words about communion, its importance and necessity. But here again all is not gold that glitters. The communion thus realized is only a caricature of a true and positive communion. The more an enslaving collectivism tries to subjugate all dominions of life, not being inclined to give room for other opinions than its own, the more we are confronted with the demoniacal face of the lust for power and of despotism. The claim of the Law of love, as here described, obviously opposes both these attitudes. From the point of view of this claim, it is not possible to take care of the fellowship without taking care of the individual, and it is not possible to take care of the individual without taking care of Society as a whole. The reason is that this universal claim is in striking and unappeasable contrast to all attempts of the aims of might to dethrone and obscure the perspective of justice. Every compromise is excluded. Justice, resting on this foundation must offer an uncompromising resistance to all tendencies that tend to degrade it, transforming it to a servant only and a slave of the interests of might. Therefore, the claim of the Law of love is the firm foundation of a "positive" communion, characterized through mutual service. "Communion" is the key-word, because the human life must be a life of communion. But at the same time, the communion cannot be attained and maintained if, for instance, the individuals are considered only as a means in the interest of the state, without regard for their condition and interests. A positive communion can be preserved only if respect for the individual is preserved, and if Society as much as possible "takes care" of its members. Here the question of "human rights" will be actualized as an object for permanent consideration. When this principle of a positive communion is the guiding idea in the life of Society, it must have the most extensive consequences for all spheres of life, for the judicial and social system as well as for education.

However, the claim of the Law concerns not only the life of the different states, but also, no less, the relations between the states and peoples. Here the most elementary manifestation of the Law could be characterized as considerateness. In a world full of all kinds of antagonisms, competitions and conflicts—nationalistic, economic, ideological, and racial conflicts—no problem can be more burning than the problem concerning the establishment and maintenance of an effective supernational order of right and justice, fighting for overcoming conflicts and destroying war. Thoroughly acquainted with all the difficulties, we know far too well that easy solutions are excluded. On the other hand, before the imminent danger of humanity, passivity and resignation must be excluded. In fact, we rather have the impression that we are now living in a period, when deep and radical revolutions are at hand, and must be at hand, that we are approaching, in one way or another, a supernational order, and that the time of the exclusive sovereignty of the nations must pass away. The problem to solve here seems to be very much the same as the problem of the relation between the community and the individual, just discussed. The goal is not to suppress the nations, but to help them to live their lives in a positive communion with each other.

The Church, considering her supernational nature as well as foremost her responsibility before the Law of the Creator, cannot elude her obligation as to the establishment of a supernational order of justice. Certainly, it is a great thing that the world has realized more and more the necessity of such an order, and that earlier failures have not deterred men from working for this purpose. Obviously, however, a primary condition for gaining a tolerable result is not only that the necessary resources of power are disposable, but also that the order of justice which can be established is supported and defended through a strong, living and vigilant sense of justice. If such a sense of justice does not exist, the endeavors are doomed to be in vain. Many different reasons may have co-operated in the failure of the League of Nations, nevertheless it may be right to say that the deepest reason was the fact that the undertaking was not supported by a sense of justice sufficiently strong to support it. From this point of view, the Church's first duty is to do all that she can to strengthen the sense of justice in the world.

Our analysis has tried to show that, from a Christian point of view, the foundation of justice is to be found in the Law of the Creator, the claim of which primarily is a careful attention to our neighbor, realized in a practical and definite way. We have emphasized that it must here be the Church's duty, no less positively than negatively, to stand up for this fundamental claim. We are then confronted with still one more question, very important for the Church's relation to Society: *the problem of the relation of Christianity to a more or less secularized humanity*. We ought to see this question, very often discussed not least in recent times, not only from a practical point of view but also from one of principle. It would be absurd if we, from our Christian outlook, did not try to find a *modus vivendi*, try to establish the contact and communion that are possible, not to say necessary, in a time of crisis. But at the same time it would be unsatisfactory to stop at practical considerations. We must also ask if there exists a principal foundation for co-operation, and in that case where this foundation is to be found.

We can scarcely deny that theology has often treated, and still often treats, this problem in a very unsatisfactory way, partly because prejudices from past days have a tendency to come back. The theological interpretations often oscillate between a radical rejection, sometimes in a rather arrogant way, and on the other side an indulgent blurredness that, trying to make contact and co-operation, more or less obscures what Christianity really is. That being so, you will easily get the impression that a positive relation between Christianity and a secularized humanism can be established only at the price of a false reinterpretation of Christianity, a price that it is not advisable to pay. A closer investigation of the radical rejection shows us that this attitude is rightly anxious not to give up the "scandalon" that belongs to Christianity, but also that this "scandalon," this offense, is easily interpreted in a wrong way, and that theology then appears with false pretensions. If theology will monopolize the sense of justice and righteousness on Christianity's account, if it will deny the "natural man's" capacity of doing anything good and useful for human society and fellowship, if it on the other side will ascribe such a capacity only to Christians, then the criticism of the secularized humanity hits the exact mark. Such a theology has, in fact, yielded to a misunderstood and false doctrine of sin, and also to a false idealization of the Christian life, and thus it has put the "scandalon" of Christianity in a wrong place.

The settlement between Christianity and a secularized humanity cannot be arranged by constructing

a communion where no communion exists, nor by concealing the possibilities of contact and co-operation that
really exist. It is not allowed to reinterpret Christianity
in order thus, as much as possible, to bring it nearer
the secularized humanity. It is necessary to let every-
thing be what it is. The difference ought not to be
concealed. The difference is foremost a difference in
the sphere of faith. The faith of a secularized humanity
is—as far as it exists—quite another than the Christian
faith, which is wholly a faith in the God who is the
Father of our Lord Jesus Christ. The possibilities of
contact and co-operation, on the other hand, lie in the
plan of the Law. The decisive question is whether we
can find any positive response for the Law claiming
careful attention to "our neighbors." Such an attitude
must be thankfully acknowledged wherever it is found.

Isn't it rather a strange idea that Christianity should
have an interest in monopolizing the sense of justice
and righteousness on its own account? Nobody reason-
ably can deny that Christian influences are to be found
even behind a radically secularized humanism. There
are of course also other influences. But the question
as regards the influences, though having a great historical interest, is in this connection irrelevant. Quite
another thing is the question of the value of an apology
that vindicates Christianity as being the only foundation of ethics and of the sense of righteousness and
thus the only basis for all endeavors towards a better
Society. It may be a temptation, especially in a time
of world-crisis, to argue in this direction. Nevertheless,
such an apology does not render any services to Chris-

tianity. Christianity has no interest in monopolizing tendencies. In fact, they are opposed to the Christian faith of creation and to the here-included conception of the Law as the universal Law of the Creator, a Law that, like the Law of the Creator, is primary also in relation to Christianity. Everybody who understands what the Law of the Creator really means must appreciate all endeavors towards a careful attention to one's neighbors and the human fellowship, whether these endeavors belong to confessing Christians or not. Here we find the principal reason why Christianity and its theology must dismiss all monopolizing tendencies, and also why Christianity must have positive relations with a more or less secularized humanism, as far as the fundamental claim is here in force. The Christian must rejoice wherever he finds the dynamical Law of the Creator in function. In fact, already, the Gospel's narrative of the Good Samaritan says the decisive and admonishing word against all isolating and monopolizing tendencies. The duty and responsibility of the Church as regards Society lies on quite another plane Her duty is, as we have already seen, first and foremost a duty to stand up for the sovereignty of the Law of the Creator. For the Church every relativizing of this Law is excluded.

VI

THE RESPONSIBILITY OF THE CHURCH

THE whole of the responsibility of the Church is defined by the fact that the Church is entrusted with the word of God. That is true also regarding the Church's relation to, and responsibility for, Society. The thought of this responsibility has been the background of all that has been said hitherto. So far we are not taking up a new subject. However, there are some concluding remarks to be made, and there ought also to be said some words about the relation between the Church's responsibility and her possibilities.

Undoubtedly the Church's sense of responsibility for Society has been strengthened in recent years. This development also has increased through influence of the world-crisis in our time. Earlier, not least in the nineteenth century, the situation on the whole was different, different also from the old days, when Christianity and Church meant so much for the construction of our social order and our civilization on the whole. However defectively the principles of Christianity were realized, nevertheless it was in those bygone days rather generally agreed that Christianity ought to be a fundamental basis of the civilization and the life of Society. On the other side, it cannot be denied that the Church in the age of the great social movements and reforms in many countries stayed very much outside the new-building forces. The impulses did not emanate from the Church, in many cases the Church rather worked as a restraining force, suspiciously looking at the development. In every case, that has been very much the situation in continental Europe—in America and in England the situation may, at least partially, have been different.

However, if the Church, more than in old times, has been isolated from the life of Society, and if also antagonism between the Church and the great social movements has arisen, how are these deplorable events to be explained? To some extent the reason of the isolation may be a distribution of the work, the fact that the state has taken charge of many duties and tasks that were earlier linked to the Church. As far as that is the case, it means at the same time that the responsibility of the state has increased. Quite another thing is the tragic fact of the antagonism between Church and labor movements that has appeared in many countries. Certainly, such movements, when following the theories of Karl Marx, declared their hostility against religion, considering it as an illusion and also as "opiate for the people." Obviously the Church could not but reject such theories, persistently repeated in leading quarters. Nevertheless we must ask if a deeper reason for the antagonism was not to be found in the Church's own attitude, in her passivity and even negativity as regards social difficulties and injustices. In fact, it cannot be denied that the Church often failed in activity as well as in clear-sightedness. However, that does not mean that the Church really had forgotten the commandment of love. In order to understand correctly the tragic situation, we must observe two things. Firstly, it seems that the Church attached too much importance to the theoretical opposition against religion. She was too apt to judge the matter only from this point of view, and did not see clearly enough that, in fact, the decisive question belonged to practical ethics. Secondly, it must be stated that the principal reason for the passivity of the Church is to be found in her individualistic interpretation of Christianity. Certainly, the Church did not forget the commandment of love. But, according to her individualistic view, this claim of the Law was considered foremost as a claim on private charity. It was not made apparent that the Law of love at the same time was a Law of justice, and that the brutal power of mammonism must be fought not only by charity, but also and foremost by creating a better order of justice in the life of Society.

Such tragic experiences and their no less tragic results have been a most severe remedy for strengthening the Church's conscience as regards the real and full sense of the Law's claim. The shock of the world-crisis came and added new incitations. We got an object-lesson, never to be forgotten. We saw clearly what the destruction of justice really meant. We saw the abyss opening its gates. There are no reasons for mitigating such a judgment. Indeed, the Nazi explosion was a unique phenomenon, a phenomenon *sui generis*. But at the same time, we shall never understand the whole scope and depth of this tragedy, if we isolate the phenomenon in question, if we do not see how it belongs to a continuity of evil forces, in which we all are partakers, not having any possibility to clear ourselves by oath. The insight into this ghastly continuity of evil forces will help us to see more clearly also the responsibility of the Church, emanating from the claim of the divine Law, as the difficulty meeting justice on its way.

The supreme difficulty is to be found in the relationship between justice and power, right and might. The situation would be easy enough if we could simply choose between might and right. But this alternative is nothing but a false simplification. In fact, we have no such possibility. Justice cannot be maintained without power in a world where strong evil forces are working. But then, there is a demon inherent in all power. Power is always tempted to misuse its position and possibilities. In our days the danger of a centralized power is so much the greater as its possibilities have increased immensely through the tremendous technical development that implies not only the most brilliant but also the most frightening perspectives. In the age of atomic power that cannot be concealed from us. In totalitarian states we have seen the demon of power unmasked. But it would be stupid to think that democratic states would be free from temptations. We know only far too well that such is not the case, that, on the contrary, totalitarian tendencies can appear also in democracies and that the life of Society as a whole is passing through a crisis where great values are at stake.

Obviously the state must possess the necessary authority. The more complicated the life of Society has become, the more impossible it is to stop at a *laissez-faire* policy. In the interest of Society as a whole, centralized planning and social control are needed. But at the same time such a planning and control involve the danger that the state will extend its power more and more and thus rule over every sphere of life.

From the point of view of the Law that the Church has to serve, two things appear as in the same degree necessary: on one side, the social order and control that belong to the careful, positive attention of "one's neighbors"; on the other side, that the attention really is a careful one, which does not suppress the individual and mechanize life. The same double-sided outlook must be applicable also to international affairs, where the world-order takes the place of the State, and the nations the place of the individuals. The line that the Church has to follow thus may be said to be clear enough—just as clear as the application will be difficult, in the various and continually changing situations. However, it is not enough to speak only about "difficulties." A realistic view of the situation shows that it is even far harder. The possibilities of realizing the claim of justice in the life of Society are always very relative. Often the fight for justice is confronted with situations where the only possibility is, either to compromise or to choose between more or less unsatisfactory alternatives. Then, the obligation of the Church in every case must be never to lose sight of the compass of justice.

Only so can the Church fulfill her task of acting as a living conscience.

To be such a living conscience of justice is the Church's primary duty in relation to Society. That does not mean that the Church should behave in any way presumptuously. The Church is not a lord of justice, but instead of that a humble servant of the justice emanating from the divine Law of the Creator. However, because this Law is a universal Law, the Church trustfully commends the claim of this Law to everybody's conscience, freely and openly co-operating with all for whom the care of justice is a holy duty.

The Church's responsibility should be reduced if only pertaining to such things as charity, reconciliation and so forth. Certainly, these functions also belong to the duty of the Church. But as regards her responsibility for Society they are secondary to the care of justice. Nothing would, as we have already indicated, be more mistaken than to separate justice from love. Justice is a legitimate child of the Law of love, its first-born child, and just as a child of love it has to lay the foundations of all human relationship.

Therefore, as regards the relation to Society, no duty of the Church can be more important than the duty of vindicating justice as supreme, as well to the state as to an over-national world-order. Bishop Berggrav, in his book *Staten og mennesket* (*State and Man*) speaks the plain truth when he says: "We do not want a stronger power of state, but a stronger justice, not a stronger 'right of might,' but a deeper respect for the right as something majestic." In fact, authority is for a state even more important than power. A state can very well increase its power and at the same time lose its authority. A state will never get real and necessary authority if it does not show respect for justice as something above the state itself. The same is true about the position of a world-order. The plain fact is that a state, when trying to extend its power over such spheres of life as justice, religion and science, exhausts the sources that are giving life and strength to the authority of the state. Then the state may increase its physical power, but at the same time it loses the authority that is most necessary for its possibilities to maintain itself and to realize its duties. Its power is an undermined power.

These considerations now lead us from the question of the Church's responsibility to the question of her possibilities to function according to her duty. The first thing then to be said is that the fundamental condition and qualification are simply that the Church remains the Church, that she remains the instrument of the Kingdom of God which she has been called to be, and thus wholly and fully to proclaim the message entrusted to her. The starting-points for all the possibilities of the Church are the mandate and mission given to her. This mandate the Church has received from her Lord. It is a gift that the Church cannot fail, without ceasing to be His Church. It is her firm and unshakable foundation. Thereby the Church has something to adhere to, something to cling to, even in times of crisis and greatest difficulties and temptations. That is the source of the Church's strength.

The mandate entrusted to the Church is the message from God, the message of the *agape* of God. Considering the Church's relation to and responsibility for Society, we have hitherto especially emphasized the Law of God. But now, regarding the message as the source of the Church's strength, we must emphasize that Law and Gospel belong together, that they are only different sides of one and the same message, and that the deepest, the real strength comes from the Gospel; that, as Luther used to say, is the highest treasure of the Church. Certainly, we can speak of a double-sided message, but finally the message is one and the same, as a message about God, about His will, about His love. His love is reflected in His Law, the Law of the Creator, but the same love in all its fullness is revealed in the Gospel, in the victorious Cross of Christ.

The Gospel, the center of which is the victorious Cross of Christ, is the deepest and most unshakable reason for our confidence, not only as regards our personal relation to God, but also as regards our outlook on history. I think we have learned that afresh during the time of the world-crisis. When looking at the continuity of the evil forces as it really appears in our world we are over and over again tempted to yield to desperation and to consider history as a meaningless process of permanent struggle. Here it is no real help to say that we ought to believe in "the goodness of man." Certainly, theology ought never to have denied that man, and even "natural man," can partially act as a servant of "the good." If man should not have such a possibility, there would not have existed any fight between good and evil in history. But such a faith in man and in his possibilities will not help us to overcome the idea of the futility of the struggle in history. Before the plain facts of history, the simple reference to "the goodness of man" will appear rather as only superficiality. And the Christians themselves will best know that we no more can base our confidence on the qualifications of the Christians—even here the fulfillment of the Law of God is a very relative one. In fact, our confidence, our conviction that history, in spite of all, is not meaningless has its basis in the revelation of the victorious Cross of Christ. Seemingly we meet here the greatest meaninglessness. But this meaninglessness is changed to the deepest meaning. That happened when Christ, when the divine Love acting through Him, went straight into the continuity of evil and, by vicarious suffering, assumed its heavy burden. Then the apparent defeat became victory. Looking steadfastly at Christus Victor and knowing that He Himself will realize His victory in the life of mankind, Faith will never cease to find a divine meaning in history. Even the evil, seeming meaningless in itself, takes on a meaning as far as it is defeated and thus forced to serve the will of God. That does not signify that the obscurity of history becomes clear. The words of St. Paul have a permanent validity: "now we see through a glass, darkly." But it means that the confidence of our faith will prevail, being based on the divine love itself and having participation in "a kingdom which cannot be moved."

However, we cannot speak about the possibilities of

the Church without more closely considering the weakness as well as the strength of the Church, her shame and her glory.

During the world-catastrophe, many Churches in different countries had grievous experiences and suffered even hard persecutions. It was a time of great trial. Now, it is not my intention to say that the time of trial would have passed. On the contrary, the present aftermath of war with all its enormous problems, difficulties, needs and claims certainly is a time of hard trial for the whole Church of Christ on earth.

Nevertheless, let us look back and ask what the black years have meant for the Church. I think *one* answer could be: the Church has gone out from the battle, that also was a time of fighting for the Church herself, with a strengthened consciousness of her own individuality, her mission and duty. That implies a sharper eye as well for her weakness as for her strength. It may perhaps be necessary to emphasize, when here speaking about the Church, that we are thinking about the actual, historical Church just as she lives on earth, just as she appears in all the different Church-communions all over the world. We will not distinguish between the institutional Church and Churches on one side, and on the other a "higher," spiritual and ideal Church. It would not be a realistic outlook if we, for instance, should refer the weakness of the Church to the institutional Church and the strength to the so-called spiritual Church. There exists no other Church than the actual, historical Church going back to Christ and His apostles and then appearing in all the different communions. Weakness and strength both belong to this actual Church of history.

It is not difficult to discover her weakness. We confess one holy Catholic Church. The Church claims to be one. But she is divided, and her divisions are infected with rivalry and antagonisms, her appearance and attitude thus reflecting the conflicts of the world. She claims to be holy. But her life is full of mistakes and sinfulness. She claims to be catholic, universal. But instead of visualizing the open Fatherly arms of God, she is often stiff and narrow-minded.

In the light of the world-tragedy, some features of the Church's weakness have been clearly elucidated. Two points ought perhaps especially to be emphasized. We have seen more obviously than ever before the real and frightening weakness of the Church's position in the so-called Christian civilization. And we have also received a new and very potent impression of the weakness, emanating from the divisions of Christendom.

Certainly, the Church has known very well for a long time past, long before the world-catastrophe, that the process of secularization was very advanced everywhere in the "Christian" countries. Nevertheless, when suddenly ideologies, openly hostile to Christianity usurped the power in great countries where Christianity had lived and worked during centuries, then it was at once unmasked how undermined the position of Christianity really was in the life of the peoples, and how far the Church had lost contact with large strata of the population, as much among the intel-

lectuals as among the working classes. But the disintegration was not confined only to these countries. It
could not be denied that the situation was very much
the same even in the nations where such revolutions
had not occurred. It may rightly be maintained that
there existed differences. Nevertheless, no nation in
the old Christendom could pretend to having no part
or lot in this advanced process of de-Christianization.
On the contrary, everywhere the Church obviously
represented only a more or less small minority. Only
some rather small circles were linked to the Church
and taking active part in her devotional life, and even
fewer would openly confess themselves as Christians.
And the Church had to a large extent accommodated
herself to this situation of isolation. That meant that
the Church to a great degree lived in her own more
or less enclosed world, and that she did not keep up
a creative contact with the centers of culture and social
endeavors. It meant also that large spheres of the old
Christendom were rather to be considered as missionary
fields.

Further, at the same time the searchlight unmerci-
fully illuminated and unmasked the canker of Christendom, consisting in her divisions, their self-content and
mutual rivalry. That was, of course, no new discovery.
But the insight into the intolerableness of the divisions
and schisms was deepened. It could not be concealed
that the possibilities of the Church to stand up for
justice and reconciliation were terribly checked by the
fact that the Church herself, through her divisions and
even antagonisms, was mixed up in the divisions, con-

flicts and antagonisms of the world. The more the Church feels her responsibility as regards the life of Society, the more she at the same time must feel the shame of her sinful weakness and the necessity of endeavors towards a deeper unity.

However, our description of the position and attitude of the Church would be one-sided and therefore at bottom false, if we should terminate with these statements and thus only speak about the weakness of the Church as it has been unmasked in the time of the world-crisis. In fact, we have also in this time of hard trial and fight acquired a new vision of the strength and glory of the Church. In the time of the First World War, the Churches on the whole remained intact, undisturbed they could discharge their duties. Nevertheless, we must with great thankfulness confess that now we have seen more of the light which shines amid the darkness and which the darkness does not overcome. Here I should like especially to emphasize three points. We have had a vision of the *inner strength* of the Church, of her *supernationalism,* of her *unity* and *universality*. But then I must immediately add that it is important not to simplify these points unduly. If we shall be able rightly to understand what has been revealed as regards the strength of the Church, we must also observe the tensions connected with these three features of the Church's life. We must see how the inner strength is connected with a strong estimation of the Church's firm constitution, how the supernationalism is connected with a clear insight as regards the Church's relation to and responsibility for the nation where she has to work, and finally how the universality and unity of the Church are connected with a confessional consciousness.

What are the source and origin of the Church's strength as appearing right through her weakness and humbleness? Nobody can hesitate about the answer. The origin of the strength is the same as it always has been, the Lord of the Church, who is the true light that the darkness cannot master. The Church's strength always depends upon her faithfulness to her Lord. As soon as this faithfulness weakens and disappears, the strength of the Church also disappears. But it would be misleading if we here yielded to a spiritualizing interpretation, if we did not see how the faithfulness in question is connected with faithfulness to the constitutive elements of the Church. Speaking about these things I will not use the words institution or organization. Such words could easily be misunderstood. Institutionalism has often been a great danger for the Church, because it easily conceals the dynamic character of the Church's message, thus leading to a bureaucratism that is a menace to the life of the Spirit. But the constitutive elements of the Church, on the other hand, are sources of life.

Considering these things we may do well once more to listen to the clear voice of the Norwegian Church, speaking in the dark night of tyranny and treachery. From whence did she get her strength? That she has openly declared: "From the Word of God." His Law gave unshakable guiding principles. His Gospel, wondrously actualized, gave power of endurance and confidence. From the sacraments. The table of the Eucharist gave communion, and baptism at once became the authority to rely upon when the power of violence wanted to force the youth to be educated in Nazi-heathenism. And one thing more: when the State-Church organization fell to pieces and the ministers of the Church were compelled to lay down their offices as far as they were related to the State, then their ordination appeared as the firm foundation of their continued service of the Church. They proclaimed: "I now divest myself of that which the State has deputed to me. The spiritual duty, assigned to me through ordination at the Lord's altar, is still mine with God and with right." You will from this illustration see how the constitutive elements of the Church appear as the firm foundation, and at the same time as source of life and action, as the dynamic of the Church: the Word of God, the sacraments and the divine mandate to be a minister in the Church of Christ.

We have also acquired a new vision of the supernationality of the Church and of her independence. We witnessed the deadly danger menacing the Church through a nationalistic constriction, oppression and superficiality. According to the statement of the Apostle that "the word of God is not bound" (II Tim. 2:9) the Church's consciousness of her independence was unshakable wherever her resistance against the oppression from the side of the state was firm. But at the same time, the Church's national and social responsibility appeared in a new and clear light. The Church must be independent in order to be able rightly to

serve the nation. The Church may be or may not be a
"national" Church. She may or she may not be connected to the state through positively organized relations. An organization where the Church is more or
less linked to the state may have its advantages as well
as it has its dangers—just as every Church organization
has advantages and dangers. A Church organized as a
national Church is not in itself unsuitable or in opposition to Christian principles. But certainly it would be
unsuitable at the moment when national relationship
is secured at the cost of the Church's freedom and
independence as regards her duty to the divine message. This independence is indispensable as far as it is
the duty of the Church always to "obey God rather
than men." The Church is not and can never be only
a department in a worldly society. Indeed, she cannot
serve the nation and the people where she lives and
works without being, and acting, as the supernational
Church of Christ.

Finally, we have indubitably acquired a new and
strengthened impression of the fact that the unity and
universality of the Church are not only an ideal, in spite
of all, but also a reality. In the first place, this unity
has appeared as co-operation. In the reports about the
actions of the Churches during the war, we have heard
from different countries how often a co-operation has
been established even between Churches that earlier
have been strictly separated and usually have looked
upon each other with considerable suspicion. In many
European countries, the Roman Catholic Church har-
moniously co-operated with Protestant Churches, de-

fending violated justice and condemning actions of brutality. I do not wish to underestimate co-operation of that kind. Indeed such workings together may be considered as promising signs. Nevertheless, two things ought to be observed. Firstly, that this co-operation was realized under very hard pressure. It could be said that the Churches were forced together by scourges. Secondly, it was a co-operation for defending the Law of God. Concord was established on the foundation of the Law. Certainly, such a concord is not to be disregarded. But at the same time, we must remember that a co-operation of this kind was not at all confined only to confessing Christians. It was also realized on a broader basis. But even if therefore the Churches ought not to boast too much of these events, on the other hand, they may be a starting-point for further and deeper co-operation. In every case they are a proof of the possibilities of the Church as regards her responsibility for the life of Society.

However, the manifestations of the Church's unity and universality have not been confined only to the co-operation now mentioned. We must thankfully acknowledge that the ecumenical endeavors in the last decades have not been futile, that indeed strong forces are here at work. The world-catastrophe separated the peoples far more than the previous world war did. Nevertheless, in spite of all difficulties, the relations between the Churches were never quite interrupted. And since the war the contacts have been taken up far more easily than in the years after 1918, when, in fact, the antagonisms also in the negotiations between the

Churches were very hard and difficult to overcome. That is a proof that the ecumenical movement has not been futile. And now we are looking forward to the great Church-Assembly of 1948, when, as we hope, the World Council of Churches will be established.

As regards the ecumenical way to a deeper and more effective unity, I think we also have a right to consider it a promising sign that theology in our days penetrates further and further the biblical message, more and more explaining it as a unity in varieties. The ecumenical aim is not uniformity. In fact, amidst all the co-operation during the hard times, the Churches did not despise their confessions. On the contrary, there is no doubt that the strength of the Churches often was connected with a rather increasing confessional self-consciousness. But such an attitude ought not to prevent an acknowledgment also of other Churches and their confessions. The evil is not the existence of different confessional Churches. It is a stiff, self-contented, doctrinarian and narrow-minded confessionalism, that, certainly, has no right in the Church of Christ. A uniformity, annihilating all differences, would mean nothing but a terrible impoverishment of the Christian Church. The biblical message, appearing as a unity in diversities, will show us the way forward. It will help us to live together in our different and beloved homes as children of the same Father, and also to recognize better the real unity of our common holy faith.

I have spoken about the Church's weakness and strength, about her shame and her glory. A realistic view must in an equal degree emphasize both these aspects. They will strengthen, each on its own account, our consciousness of the Church's responsibility. The weakness is due to the fact that the Church, living in this world, participates in its sinfulness. The strength is due to the fact that the Church "is not from hence," sharing the divine strength that "is made perfect in weakness." That is the only source of the Church's strength—but an inexhaustible source. That means that all superciliousness, all false pretensions from the side of the Church, must be condemned and excluded. But it means at the same time that the Church will work with trust and confidence—"while it is day."

INDEX

113